THE IMAGE OF LOVELINESS

THE IMAGE
OF
LOVELINESS

Joanne Wallace

Illustrations by Jan Noble

Fleming H. Revell Company
Old Tappan, New Jersey

Library of Congress Cataloging in Publication Data

Wallace, Joanne.
    The image of loveliness.

    I. Beauty, Personal. 2. Charm. 3. Etiquette for women. 4. Christian life—1960-   I. Title.
RA778.W215   646.7   78-15887
ISBN 0-8007-0963-2

To the three "gifts from God"
whom I love the most,
and who most influence my life—

My daughter, Deanna
My son, Bob
My loving, patient, and tolerant husband, Jim

Acknowledgments . . .

To Pauline Neff, whose talents translated my experiences into book form; and to Marge Nelson, Marilyn Gibson, Terri Matthews—who supported, prayed, encouraged, and worked with me diligently on the editing of the rough drafts and then added suggestions.

To my Image of Loveliness teachers, who are also my best friends.

To the thousands of students who have helped and been used in my life and have served as an inspiration. I am eternally grateful.

Contents

8 *Contents*

Foreword

For years now, ever since I wrote *The Fragrance of Beauty,* my daily mail has included a specific request from a reader—which self-improvement course I would recommend for Christian women. These questions come as no surprise. If I were asked what one problem exists in the lives of Christian women more than any other, I would say it is the lack of personal self-esteem. Not enough women really like themselves both inwardly and outwardly, and very few can understand or accept God's view of them. Ephesians 1:4 is not a reality to them—it is merely a nice verse about "someone else."

It was not until I met Joanne Wallace and heard about The Image of Loveliness that I finally found a beautifully balanced program. Joanne has neither de-emphasized the spiritual or inner beauty of women nor overstressed the outward look. She has simply designed a course—out of her love for the Lord and her modeling experience—which lovingly encourages women to take a good look at their self-worth. The expressed goal is to change what they *can* change—to become the women of God they were meant to be.

This book and course are very familiar to me. Two of my dearest friends are Image of Loveliness teachers—Clare Bauer and Teresa Landorf, my daughter-in-law—so I have firsthand knowledge about Joanne's priorities and her lovely Christ-centered guidelines.

There has never been a time when more pressure has been applied to the Christian woman—wife, mother, homemaker, divorcée, single professional—than there is today. If ever we needed a book on taking what we've been given and shaping it into the loveliest image possible—it is now! Thank you, Joanne, for just such a book.

In His Love,
JOYCE LANDORF

Introduction: God Wants You to Be Beautiful

You saw me before I was born and scheduled each day of my life before I began to breathe. Every day was recorded in your Book!

Psalms 139:16

I had never seen anything quite so beautiful as my aunt's toenails! I was twelve years old, living in Corvallis, Oregon, the day my aunt entered my bedroom and gave herself a pedicure. At first her toenails were filed straight across the top, plain-Jane fashion. They were as pale as my own. But then my aunt uncapped a bottle of nail polish and applied the ruby enamel.

Presto! The tips of her toes became as red as watermelon, gumballs and Christmas stockings hanging over a blazing fireplace. They sparkled like rockets on the Fourth of July.

What a difference that tiny bottle of polish made in my life! In my adolescent fantasies, I had pictured my world as a drab place, as plain as oatmeal. It wasn't that I didn't have wonderful Christian parents who loved me. I did. It wasn't that I couldn't wear colorful clothing, or have a room that was feminine and pink. I could. What bothered me was the women I saw at church and among my parents' friends. Not one of them wore a smidgeon of makeup or any kind of jewelry. Even the young singles had faces as pale as yesterday's mashed potatoes.

My mother was more fashionable than most in our church. She dressed in pretty, bright clothing, wore her hair short and curly, and kept her plain gold wedding ring on her finger all the time. The other mothers wore no jewelry at all. They dressed in shapeless, dowdy clothes and pulled their hair back in tight and forbidding buns.

It seemed that someone was always quoting First Timothy to me: "Women should adorn themselves modestly and sensibly in seemly apparel, not with braided hair or gold or pearls or costly attire, but by good deeds, as befits women who profess religion" (*see* 2:9).

"If you want to be beautiful, work on doing good deeds, not on fixing your face or hair," I was told. My twin sister and I told each other we could spot a Christian a mile away. Christians were the ones who made themselves look as plain and unattractive as they could. They did it on purpose.

"Charm is deceitful and beauty is vain, but a woman who fears the Lord is to be praised" (Proverbs 31:30 RSV). This was another verse I heard often at Sunday school.

The Christians I knew were good-hearted. They were clean. They were neat. But they had no outer evidence of joy. They seemed to think that telling someone they loved him was somehow improper. They talked a lot about trying to achieve something they called a "death to self." They canceled out everything I longed for— warmth, fun and beauty. Wasn't it possible that God wanted us to *look* good as well as *be* good? After all, leopards, sunsets and roses were beautiful, and He made all those. I just didn't understand.

How could it be a sin for my aunt to paint her toenails? But even as I gazed at the luscious redness, I thought about 1 Timothy 2:9 and felt anxious for her. Shouldn't she cover her toenails with the thick, wrinkly hose that all the other women I knew liked to wear? But she didn't!

Before my widening eyes, my aunt dipped her brush into the polish and touched her thumbnail with the ruby color. She went on to her index finger, and then to the middle one. By the time she had finished, all ten nails gleamed firecracker red. I looked anxiously into her eyes. I almost expected to see her transformed into something evil.

And right at that moment, I had a revelation. It was as if I were really seeing my aunt for the first time. I noticed that although she was old enough to look dowdy like the women at church, her eyes sparkled, her cheeks glowed pink. Her hair curled softly, rather than straggling from a messy bun. Her face looked soft, feminine, rounded and happy—not sallow and resigned. She laughed and gave me a hug.

I liked the way my aunt's arms felt as they encircled me. I basked in her warmth, her affection, her freedom. How could there be anything wrong with an aunt who was so loving? How could it be a sin for her to paint her toenails red?

It seemed to me that all those so-called Christians I knew were trying to be like the geodes I had seen in a souvenir shop one day. Those strange rocks were bumpy, dusty and gray on the outside. Only after they had been sawed in two could the glittering, shimmering crystals on the inside be seen.

How strange, I thought. True beauty might be only on the inside, but who in this world had the X-ray vision to penetrate such an ugly exterior? I wanted to be beautiful inside with the love of Christ, but I also wanted to be pretty on the outside, too.

As my aunt gave me her loving hug and as the fumes from the fingernail polish tantalized my nose, I made up my mind. One day, I, too, would enter the Technicolor land of cosmetics. I would paint my nails, rouge my cheeks, curl my hair. I would buy the greasiest cold cream I could find, load my lashes with mascara and spray myself with perfume you could smell from the next room. I was going to be happy inside and beautiful outside, like my aunt. What was beauty? Red fingernail polish, of course!

It was going to be much later, after several troubled years, before I finally discovered the strange balance that must exist between inner and outer beauty if a woman is to be truly attractive. I was going to have to go through a period when I felt so badly about myself that I almost ruined the lives of my children and my husband.

Only when I accepted the fact that I was made *in God's image* did I start on the long road toward being a lovely person. It is the road that led me to begin a self-improvement course, "The Image of Loveliness," that has helped thousands of women in many states learn that in order to be beautiful on the outside, they have to be filled with God inwardly. It is a road leading to continuous improvement in me. God is not through with me yet!

I want to share my discoveries with you, to help you avoid the heartaches I see every day because women deny themselves either spiritual beauty or a lovely appearance.

"Your beauty should not be *dependent* on an elaborate coiffure, or on the wearing of jewelry or fine clothes, but on the inner personality—the unfading loveliness of a calm and gentle spirit, a thing very precious in the eyes of God" (1 Peter 3:3, 4 PHILLIPS, italics mine).

God, through the Apostle Peter was warning the Christian women of his time not to copy nonbelievers. The pagan women spent all day in their palaces, braiding their hair and putting gold decorations into it, trying on luxurious fabrics and perfuming themselves from the time they woke up till they went to bed. Their minds and hearts were concerned with nothing but their appearance. So God simply said to seek the inner beauty *first,* not to neglect your appearance.

In Proverbs 31, the ideal woman is described as one who sewed for the poor, took care of her family and spoke kind words. How did she dress? ". . . her own clothing is beautifully made—a purple gown of pure linen" (Proverbs 31:22). The most expensive fabric available at that time was pure linen. The color that kings and queens often wore was purple. The Bible's ideal woman was not only industrious and good, but she also took care to make herself look as attractive as possible.

God really does want us to look lovely, because we are made in His image, and there is nothing more beautiful than Himself, His love, and His goodness.

Yet there are still many women who are as confused as I was only a few years ago. They have a faith turned wrong side out. Certain that they are ugly and unloved, they believe that there is no way that they can ever become attractive and charming. They go on living miserable, unhappy lives.

God really wants us to be like Himself so much that He made us in His own image.

The sin is not in trying to look attractive: it is in doing less than we can with what we have—a body and a personality that God wishes to be in His very own image. We fall short when we do not try to look and live our best for Him.

Believe that you can reflect His loveliness! Believe that you can become the fantastic person God wants you to be! All that is needed for you to be transformed is to accept the grace of God and discipline yourself to carry out His wishes in your life.

God likes what He has created. He wants you to like it, too!

Part I

Developing Your Personality

You are the world's light—a city on a hill, glowing in the night for all to see. Don't hide your light! Let it shine for all; let your good deeds glow for all to see, so that they will praise your heavenly Father.

Matthew 5:14–16

1

A Full Cup of Beauty

The story is told that a young man was invited to appear on TV's *The Dating Game*. He was delighted to compete for the chance to go out with one of the most beautiful girls in the nation. This young man was even more pleased when the starlet chose him to be her date for the fabulous evening that the TV network had arranged.

That night, as he watched her float in her long, shimmering gown to the chauffeured limousine that had been provided, he thought he had never seen such beauty.

However, once she was inside the car and the TV cameras had disappeared, she began to reveal her true personality. She criticized everyone, from the cameramen to the chauffeur. Inside the restaurant, she let both her date and the waiter know that the food was below her usual standards. But the most embarrassing moment of the whole evening came when she was introduced to one of the celebrities in the club. Out of her mouth poured ugly, four-letter words, which she thought would make her appear more sophisticated.

This starlet may have been photogenic, but she no longer appeared beautiful in the eyes of her date. The lovely swan with the perfect face and figure had become an ugly duckling as he watched.

Emotional responses have a great deal to do with whether or not others see us as beautiful. We all know women who by classical standards are not considered pretty. But as we learn to know them better, they seem beautiful to us. Why? They have that something extra. It may be invisible, but it affects us all the same. Some call it personality, others call it inner beauty.

Perhaps this recipe will help you understand how a girl whose looks are just average could appear to be more beautiful than a promising young starlet whose face and figure are attractive enough to secure her a spot on *The Dating Game:*

18

A Full Cup of Beauty

⅔ cup loving personality
¼ cup proper posture and positive body language
1½ tablespoons of good grooming and pleasing appearance

Mix well, and you will have plenty of beauty—enough to serve almost everyone.

Watching thousands of just-average women bloom into beautiful ladies in my classes by following that recipe, I am convinced that it works. Glow, charm, your interest in others—these are all invisible, but they represent fully two-thirds of the qualities that are essential for making others see you as beautiful. Some women naturally have a loving personality. Most of us don't. We have to work at it. Almost anyone, through self-study and a right relationship with God, can acquire one.

In my opinion, posture and positive body language represent about 25 percent of the ingredients of beauty. But I am talking about more than just the basics of sitting gracefully and standing straight. You need a way of walking that tells everyone, "I like myself." You should be able to touch a friend's shoulder in such a gentle way that you deliver the message, "I like you," without spoken words.

In fact, communications experts now believe that 60 to 80 percent of all messages are relayed nonverbally. If you make a conscious effort to send messages of love to another by leaning toward him or maintaining eye contact while he is talking, you are telling that person, "Both you and I are beautiful people."

I believe that only 10 percent of your beauty quotient depends on your grooming—your makeup, hairstyle and wardrobe selection. And if this is so, you may be wondering why so many books have been written about makeup and why American women spend millions for beauty aids. The reason is that, while a pleasing appearance may be a relatively insignificant part of beauty, *it is important*. Without it, we are like a cracker minus those few but tasty grains of salt—or the drooping houseplant that misses its tiny dollop of fertilizer.

We go by visual impressions. When a woman enters a room, we instantly form an impression. We don't wait until she utters a brilliant thought—we humans don't work that way.

If you owned a famous masterpiece, you would be sure to choose the best possible frame for it. Of course you would enjoy the painting itself (the inner part) most of all. But you would spoil the whole effect if you surrounded it with a frame that clashed in color, or looked drab, faded or peeling.

I hope you will try the suggestions that are made here, so that you may frame your inner beauty in the most attractive way. I'm excited about your prospects!

Who, Me?

You may have an endless list of excuses for why the Full Cup of Beauty formula won't work for you, but let's look at some of the more common problems and determine their validity.

Reason Number One: "How can I be beautiful when I've got this *problem?*" you say, bemoaning bow legs, a big nose, an unfortunate ability to gain weight on mere sips of water. Maybe you have thin hair, or too much hair; a bad complexion, or crooked teeth.

Sometimes we magnify our problems until they are mountains big enough to hide behind, when we could be minimizing them into molehills so tiny no one would notice. Why? It's hard work to learn to be beautiful. It is easier to give up, than to try.

Reason Number Two: "My husband wouldn't like me to change." I have found that such husbands are a rarity. The usual male reaction is one of delight.

One of my students had not warned her husband that she was going to try wearing false eyelashes. Usually when he came home for supper, he found her grubbing in the garden or cleaning up the clutter left by their three youngsters. This particular evening, when he walked in the door, he saw that she was setting the table for supper. He spotted her long, luxurious eyelashes immediately. "I like it! I like it!" he exclaimed, running toward her across the room.

Perhaps your husband may say, "You don't need a self-improvement course," or "You don't need to read a book on beauty." These words could be a compliment, but they could also mean that he cannot take the risk of seeing you become beautiful, because he has a low image of himself. He may be afraid you will become so attractive that he will lose you. (We are planning a self-improvement course for men, because so many have admitted that they, too, feel unattractive and uncertain about themselves.)

If your husband discourages you, tell him you want to learn to be beautiful inside as well as out. Explain that when this happens, you will know how to love him in a new and better way.

Reason Number Three: "Beauty is a sexist idea. If God put hair on my legs, why should I bother to remove it?" In my classes I have seen a lot of women who started out with this idea. Often they wore tailored, masculine clothes. Their expressions, hair and skin held no softness. They usually wore no makeup. In fact, they were nothing but plain!

"How I wish your classes had been available to me twenty-five years ago. Perhaps a traumatic divorce could have been avoided," said one middle-aged woman who discovered the value of femininity only after she lost her husband.

Another one of my students wrote to me, "I know there are a lot of us 'out here' who need these classes to give us a little boost in confidence and courage to accept our right and step out into a new freedom. Perhaps this is really what 'women libbers' are reaching for, without having fully defined their needs."

Reason Number Four: "I haven't the time." True, we must spend minutes, even hours, each week manicuring nails, following a skin-care program and keeping our clothes in good order if we would be beautiful. But you can learn organization that will magically stretch the hours.

Reason Number Five: "I'm not the type. Maybe others can wear paint and polish, but I'm a tomboy. Glamour is not for me." Watch it! Are these the same old negative thoughts—the inability to love and believe in yourself—putting these words in your mouth? Haven't you always secretly envied the Snow Whites in your class and the Sleeping Beauties in your neighborhood, who captured the prince just because they were lucky enough to have perfect teeth, shining hair and sparkling eyes? It is not as impossible for you to look like them as you think.

Maybe you have other reasons, ones you feel that are legitimate barriers to improving yourself. I am writing this book for you, to help you, because as a woman—God's lovely creation—it is possible for you to be beautiful in the eyes of many beholders. I have gone through all the same struggles that you are going through. And if I can improve, there is hope for anyone!

2

Fleeing the Flea Market

Believe you're a real find,
A joy to someone's heart.
You are a jewel, unique and priceless,
I don't care how you feel,
Believe it!
God *"don't make no junk!"*

No flea market for you! You are special. In fact, you are a designer's original, because when God made you, He used the pattern only once. His workmanship is better than all the dressmakers in France.

Anne Ortlund, in her outstanding book *Disciplines of the Beautiful Woman,* lovingly says, "There you are, a woman—how wonderful! How unique you are, not 'made in Japan,' but made in your mother's womb. A factory needs plenty of light; God was so smart he could make you perfectly in the dark." Woman is God's idea! How exciting!

Our wonderful Creator opens doors of opportunity, and because we don't believe in His amazing creation—ourselves—we shut the doors. When we are so centered on the self, we limit God. He is blocked because the *self* gets in the way. The Holy Spirit is not given freedom and control to work in us. All our potential is locked out.

The Reverend Donald L. Bubna (senior pastor of the church we attend, the Christian & Missionary Alliance Church in Salem, Oregon) tells a wonderful story of Mrs. Lowly and Mrs. Big that illustrates this point.

It seems that on Sunday morning, Mrs. Lowly goes to church and sees Mrs. Big standing by the door. "Wow, that woman has really got it all together," she thinks. "Just look at her grace. See how intelligent she is. She sure dresses nicely, too. Guess I'd better not even try to talk to her, because I have nothing to offer. I'll just slip out the other door so she won't see me."

While Mrs. Lowly is going out the back door (because she does not feel good enough about herself to say anything to Mrs. Big), let's listen in on the thoughts of Mrs. Big (who in her own mind is really a Mrs. Little). At this moment, Mrs. Big is offended because she just sees Mrs. Lowly (whom she thinks of as a Mrs. Large) snub her. "It's pretty obvious that lady doesn't like me," she thinks.

And that's the way we play the game that hurts ourselves and others so much. We forget that we are a Mrs. Big or a Mrs. Large, rather than a Mrs. Lowly or a Mrs. Little. We don't remember that we are made in the image of God, and are priceless to Him. But God placed such a worth upon us that He became man! He also bore our sins for us on the cross, so that we might have His righteousness. That's how worthwhile we are! Isn't that exciting!

In Matthew 22:39, Jesus says, "Love your neighbor *as much as you love yourself*" (italics added). Mark 12:31 says, "You must love others *as much as yourself*" (italics added). God really does want us to like ourselves. In fact, we cannot love our neighbors in the right way until we first love and accept ourselves.

Perhaps in your childhood your mind "tape-recorded" a message that said it was wrong to love yourself and look beautiful. Now you have to struggle to keep these old tapes from playing automatically in your head. But remember, death to self never means hating yourself. It means despising *not* yourself, but rather your selfish ways. When you ask God to take away those selfish ways, the only thing left is yourself. And God "don't make no junk!"

3

Be Kind to Yourself

Our mental institutions would not be full if more women believed that God wanted them to love, rather than hate, themselves. We've heard all our lives that it's important to be able to accept forgiveness for the things we did in the past that we didn't like. We know we are supposed to forgive others. We know that having the right attitude can help us. But how do we achieve all those qualities in ourselves?

Let's look at forgiveness first. What happens if we don't accept forgiveness for things we have done of which we are ashamed? We find ourselves playing games that Olympics committees never heard of. We become experts at "Keep Away" (avoiding others); or "Critic's Corner" (criticizing others to make ourselves feel better); "My Fault" (feeling guilty because we are jealous and envious); or "Dumb-Dumb Never" (being a perfectionist so that we can prove to everyone that we're not as stupid as we fear we are).

Or maybe we just feel worthless, like the thirteen-year-old pregnant unmarried girl who tearfully came to me after attending the Image of Loveliness class on personality. "Oh, Joanne," she sobbed. "I feel that my life is already over."

It was all I could do to keep from crying with her. My heart truly ached.

"No, it's not," I assured her with a gentle hug. "There is nothing we can do that is so wrong that God won't forgive us and make our life full and meaningful. The important thing is to agree with God that what we've done is wrong—and then to forgive ourselves. We can learn from our failures, even though they are behind us. Always remember that God wants us to try again."

"But if we confess our sins to him, he can be depended on to forgive us and to cleanse us from every wrong [and it is perfectly proper for God to do this for us because Christ died to wash away our sins]" (1 John 1:9).

You may hate your selfish ways, but you must love yourself. You can, if you honestly believe that you have God's forgiveness. In the Bible, God is praised for His tender ways of forgetting the bad things we have done. "Once again you will have compassion on us. You will tread our sins beneath your feet; you will throw them into the depths of the ocean!" (Micah 7:19).

And, as Corrie ten Boom colorfully says, "God has posted a sign which reads, 'No fishing allowed.' " I love that idea! Once we are forgiven, we are also to forget our wrongs.

To be truly beautiful, we must be able to forgive others who have hurt us. I don't believe that forgiveness will erase the memory of the past, but we will know that we are truly forgiving others when the hurt, emotion and bitterness are gone. If we consciously adopt the attitude of trying to forgive another; if we pray to God and ask Him to help us forgive someone, we will be able to do it, even when we don't feel strong enough to do it by ourselves.

"Ask, and you will be given what you ask for. Seek, and you will find. Knock, and the door will be opened" (Matthew 7:7).

Attitudes Make the Difference

Our inner attitude, reflected in smiles, the way we talk on the phone, the way we say, "Hi!" can make us appear either beautiful or unattractive to others. This can affect all our daily living.

Because I am a night person, morning is my least favorite time of the day. When I am stumbling around in my prebreakfast fog, God gives me the choice of being pleasant and greeting my family in the kitchen with a smile—or with a grumble. I have to choose which attitudes I will adopt for the day. Sometimes my family tells me tactfully that I have *selected* a grouchy attitude before breakfast. They tease me by quoting Proverbs 27:14: "If you *shout* a pleasant greeting to a friend too early in the morning, he will count it as a curse!" I know right away that my attitude needs changing!

After attending the class on personality, one of my students decided that from then on, her attitudes would be perfect. The next morning she was cheerful for at least five minutes after the alarm rang. Then the children started yelling, and she lost her temper and yelled back. She could have become very discouraged and never tried again.

"But," this woman told me, "I began to realize that God loved me very much, and that He had control of my every breath. As He gave me another breath, it was almost as if He were saying, 'Here, child; I love you. Try again.' "

Depression—Who Needs It?

Sometimes when we are really unhappy with ourselves, it is very hard to refrain from taking our bad feelings out on others. We may recognize that our attitude is bad, but we feel too defeated to do anything but nurse our hurts. If you find that you are depressed, you may still be able to coax yourself into being pleasant to others. If you do, you will feel better.

Dr. Paul Gillette, coauthor of *Depression, A Layman's Guide to the Symptoms and Cures,* advises, "Get out of the house. Go to a movie, a concert, a ball game. Call a friend you trust and talk about some of your worries. Do something for somebody."

I'll vote especially for the last bit of advice. Volunteers are always needed in hospitals, your church and civic groups. Or you can simply do something for somebody on a one-to-one basis. You will look and feel much more beautiful.

One of my students decided that she would bake a chocolate pie and take it to the women who worked in her husband's office. "In my depression, I hated everyone so much that I could barely keep myself from substituting a laxative for the chocolate in the recipe," she admitted. "Instead, I forced myself to make the best pie I could. I dragged myself into the car and drove to the office. Then, as I walked into the building and saw how cute and attractive the receptionist was, I had a horrible impulse. I found myself wanting to throw the pie at her! But I didn't. I handed it to her and said in a grumbling tone, 'This is for you and the rest of the office staff.' Immediately everyone gathered around me and oohed and aahed over that chocolate pie—far more than it deserved," she said. "I left walking on air. I was a different woman all day."

Our daughter Deanna decided when she was a sophomore in high school that she should be doing some type of volunteer work. So she became a candy striper at a local hospital. As she delivered flowers and cards to lonely patients or read a letter to a person with bandaged eyes, she received overwhelming appreciation.

Her happiness came not because she was being paid to do it (she wasn't); but from sharing herself. We don't become happy by doing what *we want,* but by sharing our gifts freely with others. Deanna is learning that in serving others, she can become a very beautiful young lady.

4

Fears Versus Tears

It is easy to see that we are unattractive to others when we are afraid to take the first steps toward being positive and outgoing. But tears may sometimes demonstrate your gentleness—a quality the world appreciates.

Let's look first at how fears can make you seem unattractive to others. Maybe you want to be positive and smiling when you walk into a room full of people. But you're afraid. You flatten yourself against a comforting wall and stay there all evening.

Or maybe you want to try to be elected club president or promoted to manager of the office. But your body and mind seem tied with icy ropes. The awful thought keeps coming back: what if I try—and then fail? It is easier to sit back and feel negative (and unattractive) in lonely, insecure misery than to risk defeat.

At one time I was afraid to try to do anything. Somewhere in my growing-up years I got the mistaken notion that the best thing to do, if you feel you can't achieve a certain goal, is just to accept the fact and adjust to the situation. Only after I began the process of accepting myself, did I begin consciously trying to change my attitude toward risk taking. I took a big step forward when I competed for the Mrs. America contest and was rewarded with the crown of Mrs. Oregon. I wished that I had known a long time ago that it was far better to risk and fail than never to try at all.

When my son Bob decided that he wanted to be president of the seventh grade class, Jim and I encouraged him to campaign. We knew that he might lose the election. But if he did, it would be far better than having to hear him say, as I have said many times, "If only I had tried, I might have made it."

Bob ran for class president in the seventh grade and lost. He tried again in the eighth and ninth grades without success. Not until he was in the tenth grade did he win! In his senior year of high school, he became student-body president, simply because he began trying to win way back in the seventh grade.

Deanna entered five beauty pageants before she won a title and competed in the Miss Oregon Scholarship Pageant (a preliminary to Miss America). Jim and I are proud of both of our children—more because they kept trying and did not get discouraged, than that they finally won.

If there is something you want to do, but you feel fear gripping you, that is the very time you must force yourself to act.

When Jim wanted our whole family to fly to Chicago with him in a little four-place airplane, I was terribly afraid. I did not fear commercial flights, but this tiny plane seemed like nothing more than a child's toy. I was sure we would all be killed. But Jim had his heart set on piloting us. So after a lot of praying, I forced myself to say yes.

Our journey required three days, because we had several stops to make. Every morning, as my stomach somersaulted on the takeoff, the tears would roll down my face. I kept thinking of the Scripture, "Lo, I am with you always." Did that mean "Low (on the ground) I am with you, but not up in this flimsy airplane"? I couldn't help thinking it did.

"Why are you crying?" Jim kept asking me.

"Because I'm chicken!" I wailed. I didn't see how Jim could help but get lost up there without a road map. I knew the plane would malfunction. When we arrived in Chicago without a single problem, I was almost shocked. Only then did I begin to enjoy myself. On the journey home, my tears did not flow a single time. By forcing myself to do something of which I was deathly afraid, I had conquered my fear of it.

"God has not given us a spirit of fear, but of power and of love and a sound mind" (*see* 2 Timothy 1:7). This is a verse I try to remember when I am afraid.

If you are scared, or sad, or even very happy, you may feel the urge to cry. If you do, let the tears roll. We can't have control of our emotions all the time. Naturally you should not go around boo-hooing on every shoulder you find. This kind of crying could be an urge to get attention. But don't be afraid to shed tears at appropriate times. Letting out emotions through tears helps our mental health, and crying can be one of the greatest things in the world to relieve emotional tension.

One lady in my classes had been married for thirty years and had never squeezed out a single tear since she had been taught as a child that "big girls don't cry." What she did not realize was that her harshness was visible. It destroyed her inner beauty. She scarcely ever talked to anyone, and consequently she had few friends. When I pointed out in class that crying is not a weakness, she began at certain times to let her tears flow. She is now developing a genuine softness that is much more appealing than was her stoic reserve.

Most men seem to feel that they have to fight tears. Perhaps they don't realize that Galatians 5:22 lists *gentleness* as one fruit of the spirit. This Scripture applies to men as well as women. Physicians tell us that men die with heart troubles and ulcers many years before women do, and one possible reason is that our society has not allowed them to shed tears.

Like most males, my teenaged son Bob thought he would be considered a sissy if he wept. Once he invited a girl to watch TV with him. The movie was a sad one. Soon Bob was in the kitchen, looking panic-stricken.

"Mom!" he said in a broken voice. "She's crying."

"Does that bother you?" I asked.

"Yes," he blurted out. "She might make me cry, too."

If you cry when you hear beautiful music, you are demonstrating your humanness. Don't apologize! The world will be happy to see that you have tenderness.

I wish that you could go to a salon and have your personality colored just as you like it, all in one single afternoon. But you can't. It takes time to develop a beautiful inner you. The only way to make it happen is to start trying right now. I hope that someday you, too, will view yourself as did Leona Ambrose, a student of Carol Brockway, Image of Loveliness teacher in Twin Falls, Idaho:

I See Myself As God Sees Me!

1. Original—one of a kind—unique!
2. I was made in the image of God—to make His image visible.
3. God has a plan for my life!
4. I thank God for working with me this far.
5. I will stop knocking myself (criticizing my Creator!).
6. My appearance reveals that God's reputation is at stake!
7. I will work on developing inward qualities to be beautiful inside.
8. I cannot be inferior without my own consent!
9. I want to change—for abundant living!
10. I will accept myself—God is not finished with me yet!

Assignment: Develop Your Personality

1. Stand before a full-length mirror. Start with the top of your head and let your eyes travel over your whole body, giving thanks to God for every part of it. (Don't thank Him that you are not worse than you are!) Thank Him for everything—including bad backs, large noses and freckles. Accept your own special gifts, your vocation, your opportunities, your health or your lack of health. Realize that acceptance brings freedom to be the person God wants and plans for you to be. And remember that God is still fashioning you. He is not through with you yet.

2. Read Psalms 139:14–19 in the Living Bible. Thank God that He thinks about you always.

3. Meditate daily on the kind of person you want to be. Picture yourself doing the things that are happy, confident and gentle. Ask your heavenly Father's help in becoming the person He wants you to be.

4. Do something good for somebody today, without being asked, and don't tell anybody else that you did it. If you tell, don't count it for this assignment.

Part II

Graciousness

If I had the gift of prophecy and knew all about what is going to happen in the future, knew everything about everything, but didn't love others, what good would it do?

1 Corinthians 13:2

5

Rabbits in Your Hat

Sir James Barrie defines the inner glow that is so often described as charm in this way: "Charm is a sort of a bloom on a woman. When she has it, she doesn't need anything else. If she doesn't have it, nothing else matters."

Does it require magic to achieve that kind of beauty? No. We all know that rabbits don't appear in hats at the wave of a wand unless they are put there ahead of time. And that's not magic. It's called planning ahead. Why not plan to put more charming traits into *your* "hat" today!

First let's look at tact, or the ability to offer suggestions and comments to others in a diplomatic way. Sometimes it seems very difficult to be tactful. We can see so clearly that our best friend could easily improve her marriage if she stopped nagging her husband, and we feel we ought to tell her so. If we don't use a bushel of tact in telling her, she will feel a ton of disapproval. She will end up feeling worse about herself than she already does, and she won't see us as beautiful at all. "It is harder to win back the friendship of an offended brother than to capture a fortified city. His anger shuts you out like iron bars" (Proverbs 18:19).

I stress the learning of tact so much that two of my teachers once wrote a little skit spoofing me at a training meeting. Joan Wallace (who is no kin to me, despite the similarity of names) took the role of The Image of Loveliness doll. When Suzy Willhite wound up the big key in her back, Joan said in a robot-like voice, "I am an Image of Loveliness doll, and I am tactful."

"Oh, really?" said Suzy. "And what can you say that is tactful?"

The doll opened her mouth, and out came—"You don't sweat much, for a fat lady."

All the teachers roared. This doll had the concept of being tactful, but she used it in the wrong way. Joan made Suzy feel good about herself ("You don't sweat much"), but her implied suggestion that Suzy go on a diet ("for a fat lady") was far from diplomatic.

A tactful person always thinks first of the feelings of others. If the truth is too blunt, she says nothing. Above all else, she is kind. Be sure that your suggestions do not reflect your own intolerance. Many times others will have ideas that are different from your own, which may be perfectly legitimate.

Gray at Twenty-one

It has been said that it takes four positive statements to neutralize the effects of every negative comment that we hear about ourselves. It is as if we are born as a bucket of white paint. Throughout our lives, we come in contact with plenty of negative people, who keep dropping black specks into our white. By the time we are twenty-one, some of us are very gray.

Have you ever said, "I'm so stupid I can't do anything right"? Or, "I don't have any talent at all." Or, "Guess I can't expect to have a date, like the pretty girls." If you have, then you are dropping black specks of paint into your own white bucket. You are criticizing the fantastic job that God performed when He made you in His image. We need to learn to consciously avoid knocking ourselves. How many black specks have we dropped into someone else's bucket of white?

Joyce Landorf, in her book *The Fragrance of Beauty,* urges us all to adopt what she calls a "no-knock" policy. Every time you would downgrade yourself, your mate, your children, a neighbor, a friend or business acquaintance, she urges you to refuse to say the words.

Sometimes we don't realize we are saying damaging words. When I was a child, my brother and sisters seemed to me to be quiet and dignified children. But not *me!* In fact, I couldn't sit still. When we had company, I would jump, run and stand on the piano stool. Sitting still was an impossibility. Friends and relatives used to shake their heads, laugh and say, "Wow, Joanne is really the odd one. If anyone is going to be different or cause trouble, it's got to be Joanne."

They didn't mean to be negative toward me. Being a parent myself now, I can understand their frustration! But in my childhood, I began to feel that I was very odd indeed. In fact, when I was thirteen, I used to go into the bathroom and lock the door. I would stare in a mirror, squinching up my eyes and trying to blush as hard as I could. Why? My twin sister blushed easily, and I couldn't. My friends had teased me about it, and I thought there must be something wrong with me. I didn't have too much trouble from these negative feelings about myself until after I was married. That is when the seeds that were planted so long ago bloomed into a kind of ragweed to which I was definitely allergic.

Ethel Barrett in *Don't Look Now But Your Personality Is Showing,* says, "We would worry less what others think of us if we realized how seldom they do." But as we are growing up, we don't understand that. Children are supersensitive to criticism.

If you have children, abolish jokes like, "Oh, Billy, you're my little monster." If Billy thinks he is a monster, he acts like one. Instead, compliment your children. They can never hear too many good things about themselves. Neither can anyone else! And that includes you.

Think back to the last time someone gave you a compliment. Did you accept it or reject it? If we squelch a compliment, we do not prove our modesty. We actually insult the giver, who wanted to express a word of love to us. We reject the very lifeblood we need to survive as a human being.

Unfortunately most women seem to accept complaints more graciously than they do compliments. How many times has someone told you your dress was pretty and you said, "Oh, this old thing? I've had it for years." Or, "It's awful. It makes my hips look so big." When you say that, everyone immediately inspects your hips and nods a head. "Good grief! She is right. I never noticed it before, but her hips are big!"

If you receive a compliment, accept it. Recognize that the giver wants you to feel good about yourself. A simple "Thank you. I'm glad you like it" is a wonderful response that makes both of you feel more beautiful.

When Bob was ten, he used one finger to laboriously type this message for me one day when I was particularly busy: "Thankyou Mother. Thankyou Mother For Loving Me; Thankyou Mother For Caring for Me; Thankyou For Your Care & Kindness, Even When You Have Some Business; *I Love You!*" Needless to stay, I still have that beautiful compliment tucked away in my memory book.

After he was about fourteen, Bob often stopped telling me he loved me. Instead he would say, "Oh, Mom, you sure look pretty."

He would even give me such compliments at 7:00 A.M., as I stumbled sleepily around the kitchen making breakfast. Finally one morning I yelled at him, "I do not look pretty. What's the matter with you!"

Bob ran into the living room, his face contorted with misery. "Don't you realize, Mom, that when I say those things, it's just like saying 'I love you'?" Bob had reached the age when it was hard for him to say, "I love you." His compliments were simply an attempt to communicate his love. What did I do? I rejected him! We should all recognize that a compliment is a word of love. It's a miracle, which can turn a spoonful of quinine into fresh strawberry pie.

Some people feel so insulted when their compliments are rejected that they stop giving them. It hurts when that happens, of course. But sometimes we have to risk rejection if we want to be beautiful. One student told me she had not told her husband she loved him in twenty years.

"Why not?" I asked.

"He stopped saying 'I love you,' so I did, too!" she explained. How my heart ached for that woman. Her selfishness would not allow her to risk giving something without receiving something in return. It was likely that she would never know the joy of receiving her husband's love.

It is true that many men are as shy about accepting compliments as giving them. But, as one of my students learned (because she was determined to take the risk), there is a tactful way of giving a compliment to a husband who is not too communicative. While watching TV with him, she noticed his arm lying on his knee. The arm was rather thin, but hairy. She leaned toward him and said, "I just love your arm—it's so masculine."

Her husband looked embarrassed and jerked his arm away. "No, it's not," he said and hurriedly put it in his lap. But during the evening, she noticed he kept bringing his arm up and inspecting it when he thought she was not looking!

I know a twelve-year-old girl who couldn't bear to tell her father she loved him. No one in that family had talked about love for years. "If I say I love him, he will just think I want him to give me money for a new dress," she argued. But finally she decided to take a chance. She wrote on a piece of paper, "I love you. Lane." Then she laid the paper on her parents' bed.

Her father found it and was thrilled. Then, while he was taking a shower, his wife found the note and thought it was for her. The next day, both the mother and father told their daughter they loved her. That family has a new and wonderful relationship, simply because she had not followed the "safer" path of never writing anything at all.

6

Freeing the Butterfly

We all need to know that we are appreciated and loved, so we should say these sentences to at least one other person every day:

1. I love you.
2. I appreciate you.
3. I'm proud of you.

By saying these words, we can help others bleach out the black spots in their buckets of white paint. Remember that it takes four positives to cancel out one negative? If all those people with whom we daily come in contact are going to be able to escape the cocoons of daily sameness and drudgery in which they are sealed, they will need our help.

Think about your children's teachers, your beautician, the neighbor who drives in your car pool. Are you taking their work for granted? Maybe they're just waiting to hear someone say, "I appreciate you," so that they can come out of their cocoons and become the beautiful butterflies they were meant to be!

Why not make a telephone call to say you love them, or send a note with a sentence of appreciation? Maybe you think they have already heard enough good things about themselves. But even if they know they've done some good things, they can never hear your words of love too many times.

And what about the people who haven't really done anything for you, but who are weighted down with problems and need your encouragement? They may be desperate to hear from you.

One woman told me she didn't have time to take The Image of Loveliness course, because she was going through a divorce. It was obvious that things were not going well with her.

After hanging up the phone, I felt a cloud of sadness lurking over me. I found a friendship card that had an appropriate poem on it and wrote to her: "I talked with you on the phone today and trust that things are going well. Just wanted to let you know that I care. Love, Joanne."

She called me the next day and sobbed, "I'm alive today because you said you cared." She had planned to take her own life, and it was God's perfect timing to have the mailman deliver my card before she slipped into a Christless eternity.

This incident prompted me to ask the Lord to help me be more sensitive to His Spirit's prodding, so that I'll always carry out my good intentions instead of letting some slip away unaccomplished. It has been said that good intentions are not *good* until they are carried out!

A gracious person always keeps a supply of notes in her cupboard, sending them generously. Writing these messages of love can help fight our own depression. One of our students felt she just wasn't growing as she wanted to. I could see that she was suffering from the blahs—that feeling of *Why get up and get dressed, when I have to go to bed again tonight?* I suggested that she write some appreciation notes that very day. She called that night to say she had written seventeen notes and felt much better.

It is not necessary to write that many. And you shouldn't write them with the idea that by complimenting someone else you can manipulate them into doing what you want them to do for you. But do write unselfishly, to help someone else.

Some of you may be saying, "I don't have time to write appreciation notes. It's all I can do to accomplish the basics around the house. I am so busy!" I know how you feel, as we all are busy people, but we also all have the same amount of time!

The answer is to become organized. Before you go to bed at night, make a list of all the things you have to do tomorrow. You will then be able to sleep well, because everything is securely written down on paper. This will help eliminate waking up in the middle of the night thinking, *I must remember to go to the cleaners tomorrow.* As you accomplish each task, cross it off your list. You may not finish everything, but you will probably accomplish a great deal more than you expected.

Your husband and children may also appreciate having you write down the things you would like *them* to do. One woman told me she makes such a list for her husband and puts it on the bulletin board. Then, when and if he wishes to accomplish a task, he does it. She said that this eliminates nagging.

I was interested to read in Proverbs 31:15, in regard to the description of the godly woman, that she "gives portions to her maidens," and in the New American Standard Bible there is a note that this Scripture means that she gives "prescribed tasks."

A Star Is Born

Being gracious is, of course, a lot more than being tactful, learning to give and receive compliments, and showing appreciation and love to others.

Because you are interested enough to read this book, you will probably try to make the effort to be charming and beautiful, no matter where you go. However, one of our students wore hair rollers to every class session. "I just can't do anything with my hair, so I keep it up in rollers," she explained. I needed a lot of tact to let her know that rollers are far from attractive as a hairdo. Fortunately, our hair-care class soon solved many of her problems. What a thrill it was to see her with a good basic haircut, shining with a real aura of beauty!

We aren't saying that you should never put rollers in your hair. Many of us have to do that, but we should remove our hair curlers if we plan to go anywhere outside of our own home (or car). Perhaps you must drive your husband to work at 7:00 A.M. and you don't have time for a comb-out, figuring you can get by at that time of morning. Maybe you can—if you have your head covered with a scarf and don't stop along the way for milk. You *could* meet someone you know and want to do a disappearing act.

To avoid having to run to the store when they do not look presentable, we suggest to our students that they try to keep extra food on hand. We also stress the importance of being organized in every area of life as a means of becoming a lovelier person.

After talking about being organized, one student decided that she would make it a point to keep extra snack food around the house, in case unexpected company arrived. She successfully stored an extra roast in her refrigerator, but homemade cookies were another thing! Her children seemed to develop strange radarlike capabilities for finding them. The goodies would be gone by the end of the day. One day she used her ingenuity and put the cookies in the freezer, in a container labeled "peas."

Be "loveliness" conscious and practice being a beautiful person—a "star" in whatever your circumstances. Always remember that you are special to God because He made you in His image.

Reach Out

I encourage you to develop your talents for being tactful and organized—but by all means, keep your sense of humor. Learn to reach out to others and express your love, reflecting that special glow that will make you irresistible.

Assignment: Graciousness

1. Buy a box of cards that would be suitable for writing an appreciation note. Mark your calendar with a notation to send at least one appreciation note each week. *Be sure that you write it!*

2. Think of some quality or act done by five of your best friends and members of your family that merits a compliment. Then tell them *today* what it is you like about them. *Say it out loud!*

3. Accept the next compliment you receive with a simple "Thank you—I appreciate that."

Part III

Body Language

And so, dear brothers, I plead with you to give your bodies to God. Let them be a living sacrifice, holy—the kind he can accept. When you think of what he has done for you, is this too much to ask? Don't copy the behavior and customs of this world, but be a new and different person with a fresh newness in all you do and think. Then you will learn from your own experience how his ways will really satisfy you.

Romans 12:1, 2

7

Let Your Face Talk!

A minister looked out at his congregation on Sunday morning and said, "I know there are lots of happy, joyous people here this morning." He paused a minute and then went on. "I just wish they'd notify their faces." Whoops! The congregation's body language was showing. The pastor, without seeing any smiles, could not feel his flock's happiness.

Others can be drawn to us through our body language—which includes walking, sitting and standing properly. We can also lose one to two inches in the waist and hips, if need be, simply by practicing correct posture. Our clothes will look better, too.

In The Image of Loveliness classes, much time is spent in each session in drilling students on the correct way to stand, sit and walk. We will study some of these basics in this book, because you will want to have that extra beauty bonus of perfect posture.

But first, let's look at how body language can affect your appearance. Almost everyone I know is concerned to some degree with looking interesting and attractive to others. Yet many are labeled "expendable" even before they open their mouths. How can this happen?

Let's say a new member of your club is introduced to you. She slouches on one leg, letting her shoulders slump dejectedly. While being presented to you, she takes a step backward, without even smiling. Her eyes focus *not on you,* but on a spot on the wall over your left shoulder.

"What an aloof person!" you are thinking. "She's trying to freeze me out—probably thinks she's better than I am." But you are wrong. Like Mrs. Lowly, this woman wants your friendship more than anything but doesn't know how to receive it.

Our body language also includes the movement of our eyes and our hands, the glow or dullness in our faces. It is a universal language that says everything about our acceptance or rejection of ourselves and others. To a certain extent, we all can understand it, but sometimes we send out garbled messages.

When counselors and psychologists tell us that 60 to 80 percent of all communication is nonverbal, they mean that we are often saying more with our bodies than with our tongues. Nothing is wrong with that, if we like ourselves, for our bodies will faithfully report that fact. But if we don't accept ourselves, if we feel anxious or worthless, our bodies automatically deliver that message, too.

If you have days when you feel like a Mrs. Lowly, don't despair. Just as you can learn to speak French by studying it from a book and then practicing, you can also become fluent in the kind of body language that says, "I like myself, and I also like you." As you act out this self-confident behavior, you will almost miraculously come to like yourself better. I wish I could see the wonderful changes that are going to be made in you!

Right Face, March!

Has anyone ever said to you, after he or she had known you for a long time, "I used to think you were stuck on yourself"; or "At first I thought you didn't like me"; or "It took me a long time to realize you were so nice"?

If so, you might consider what facial expressions can do to you. See if you can spot yourself from among my collection of friends that follows, all of whom are woefully ignorant of the negative messages they are transmitting with their faces.

Betty Blah. Where is her mind? It must be at least a million miles away. "There's certainly nothing interesting around here," she seems to be saying—and no wonder! Who will speak to this lady when she wears such an expression? She's telling everyone she isn't interested in anything.

Martyred Marcie. "Why must I suffer?" says her expression. "I'm bored. Everything around here is painfully dull and dead." Everyone is bound to avoid Marcie as if she had Legionnaire's Disease.

Drop-Dead Donna. "I don't like you any better than you like me," her face says. If your husband looks at a pretty girl a fraction of a second too long, your face may wear this expression, too. The poor girl then figures that you really don't like her, so she retaliates with her own "drop dead" look. War is declared and casualties mount.

Nose-Tilt Nanette. "Sorry, the rest of you don't have what I've got," says this lady, who definitely seems to feel superior to all in the room. Would you believe she really is covering up for her own sense of inferiority? If we like and accept ourselves, we won't get trapped into a nose-tilting contest. When we try to show everyone else how great we are, we may be pushing away what we need most—love!

Come-Close Corinne. Note how the corners of her mouth turn up, not down. Her eyes seem to have a warm, kind, loving sparkle. Her inner loveliness bubbles out all over her face. No wonder we all want to be with her!

What thought now comes to mind? Did we see all our friends' faces, or did we see our own? Most of us who never really studied our own expressions have to admit that sometimes we look like at least one of the first four caricatures. Often not like Corinne!

For some of us, smiling is not easy, but it can be learned. In The Image of Loveliness classes, we take time out to do facial exercises, so that we can erase any hint of a Betty Blah or a Drop-Dead Donna. Remember, a smile is the most important thing a woman can wear!

You can learn to smile, and you are going to look wonderful when you do! Some people I know have crooked teeth or a gap between molars—at every laugh or agreeable expression, they throw a hand in front of their mouth to try to cover up their defects. They don't realize that their hand works like a great big pointer, alerting others to the fact that there is a terrible secret hidden there.

If you are truly self-conscious about your teeth, then go to a good dentist and have them capped or straightened, no matter what your age. If you can't do that, accept your teeth. Tie your hands to your sides, if you must, to keep them from flying to your mouth. Almost certainly your tooth problem is not as great as you think it is. If you don't point it out, few will notice.

We all have parts of our body that we like better than other parts. Almost everyone can open up her Bluebeard's closet and bring out a favorite horror. In my classes some shudder over bow legs, others flinch because of swaybacks or squinty eyes. There are ways to diminish the effect of all these physical monsters that seem to drain away our self-confidence, however. Students who have spent a lifetime bemoaning their terrible teeth often discover in our classes that hardly anybody ever really noticed them before. All over the room I hear comments such as "Where are your teeth crooked? Oh, you mean that little place there? That's nothing. I never noticed it before."

Something else to remember about smiles is that gum chewing can be offensive and distracting to others and can detract from your smile. If you have bad-breath problems, be sure to brush often, following with a good mouth freshener. (In fact, it's a good idea for all of us to make use of one.)

How else can we train our faces to deliver good, positive messages to others? We need to listen actively. As others talk, let your face be pleasant, a reflection of your reactions (unless you are angry!). Keep your eyes focused on the speaker's eyes, to let him know he has your complete attention. But don't wear a glassy stare.

Blink often and alter your eye and mouth expressions to suit the changing subjects of conversation.

Some people like to throw their heads about for emphasis as they are talking. These athletics are as distracting as trying to carry on a conversation while watching a tennis game. Teach your head to remain still. It's your face that should provide the action. No matter how much you practice body language, however, the best assurance that your face will always be saying, "I like you," to others is by accepting yourself. So work on the inner you.

Proverbs 15:13 says, "A merry heart maketh a cheerful countenance . . ." (KJV). The Living Bible puts it this way, "A happy face means a glad heart . . . ." Remember that inner purity will *automatically* bring to your face the cheerful, sunny look that you desire.

Jesus said, "So watch out that the sunshine isn't blotted out. If you are filled with light within, with no dark corners, then your face will be radiant too, as though a floodlight is beamed upon you" (Luke 11:35, 36).

8

Bodies Have a Message, Too

Facial expressions are important in delivering the message that you love others. But the rest of your body also speaks loudly and clearly.

When my daughter was in high school, she didn't think that the boys liked her at all (although she has always been beautiful!). "When they talk to me, they look out the window, rather than at me. Their eyes travel all around the room. They tug at their shirts, squirm and appear to be bored to death if I speak to them," she said.

It was not until after she went to college that she realized that some of these boys had probably squirmed because they were shy and insecure and they wanted to make a good impression so badly that they didn't dare let her know how interested they really were. But then again, some of them may just have had other interests.

If you are speaking body language with the same kind of misleading accent, don't despair. As you learn to improve your outer appearance with the right makeup and hairstyle, you will also gain a better feeling about yourself. As you practice listening attentively or leaning toward someone, rather than away from him, your body language will improve.

A Bible study teacher had a very beautiful girl in her group. This girl had the perfect figure, long slender fingers and a classic face. But no matter what anyone said, she could not accept herself as being beautiful, and her body language told the tale. One day in private, the loving teacher stood her in front of a mirror and asked her to look at herself.

"Say, 'I'm beautiful,' " coaxed the teacher tenderly. The girl refused. She just didn't feel beautiful on the inside. Without overcoming the girl's inner self-rejection, there was little the teacher could do to improve her shyness, her slumping shoulders and grim expression.

Try to develop enthusiasm, for this quality automatically creates pleasant body language. Did you know that the Greek from which this word stems (*En Theos*) means "God within you"? No matter what kind of personality you have, enthusiasm makes it better! It provides you with God's power to motivate others!

How does enthusiasm work? One woman attends a sale of beautiful sweaters marked down amazingly low in price. She tells her neighbor in a dull, monotonous voice, "There is a sale downtown. A lot of sweaters are out on tables, and they're marked down."

Little that she says will excite her neighbor to want to see these bargains. But if her eyes sparkle, her face lights up and she says, "Macy's has the most beautiful sweaters on sale downtown! I can't believe it! They are marked down to only five-ninety-nine . . ." she won't be able to stop her friend from rushing to the store. Enthusiasm makes the difference! It's as contagious as chicken pox and a whole lot nicer.

Stop Me If You've Heard This One

How many times have you heard that you should stand tall, with your tummy tucked in, shoulders straight and head level? "Oh, you mean posture? I heard all about that in junior high." Probably you did. But what I see so often is that few actually practice what's been preached so often. You can look so much lovelier if you practice good posture each day.

Postures on Parade

Listen, my children, and let me talk
Of the dreadful ways that ladies walk;
Look, while we show you a style parade
Of ladies doing a promenade
Just to illustrate, all in fun,
How your walking should *not* be done,
Horrible samples will soon appear,
Who by posture will make it clear
Just what happens to women fair
Who do not know or who do not care
How they look when they take the air.
Stop, look, listen, and tremble, too.
Do these walkers resemble *you?*

Sylvia Slouch

First with a slinky backward
    crouch
Enters Debutante Sylvia Slouch.
Up with hips and down with
    seat,
Here is Sylvia, all complete.
Saggy shoulders and sunken
    chest,
Poor old diaphragm quite de-
    pressed,
Who is Sylvia—she's a sight!
She could be pretty if she walked
    upright.

Susie Swayback

Next we beg to introduce
Susie Swayback, on the loose.
Sue is full of curves and graces,
But she curves in frightful
    places.
See the hollow in her spine.
Note the most distressing line
From her chin down to her
    shoesies,
Ah, the streets are full of Susies!

Hortense Hump

Here's a dowager, sleek and
    plump,
Cursed with a dowager's famous
    hump.
Lots of dowagers get like that
When they're lazy, and rich and
    fat.
Is it something that she ate
Or because she won't stand
    straight?
Humps belong on camels,
    madam,
Ladies never should have had
    'em!

Samantha Stoop

Down the street with a sort of
    droop,
Here comes trotting Samantha
    Stoop.
Here is a student who loves her
    books.
(Oh, how study can ruin looks!)
Shoulders stooping and head
    out-thrust,
Laugh if you will and weep if
    you must.
Wherever she goes, in thought
    immersed,
Her legs go last and her nose
    goes first!

Sally Stiff

Parades, of course, are lots of fun.
But what girl wishes to walk like one?
Yet Sally Stiff, the crazy nut,
Has got a military strut.
With shoulders stiff and backbone rigid,
She has a gait that's simply frigid.
If the army saw her, they'd enlist her,
But where's the man who's ever kissed
  her?

Conclusion . . .

Now that we've tactfully put on the spot,
Ladies who walk as they plainly should not,
If our review is to do any good, we'll now
Show someone who walks as she *should!*
So in conclusion, we're pleased to present,
Miss Polly Posture, a maid heaven-sent,
Easy and graceful, natural and fine,
Showing respect for her chest and her
  spine.
All of her inwards in perfect alignment,
Here is the essence of grace and refine-
  ment.
Do you observe, as she comes into view,
She walks exactly, precisely like *you?*

Here's an easy way to see if your body lines up properly when you stand. Tape a six-foot long string to a full-length mirror and weight it with a heavy object that will keep it taut. Then line your body up with the string.

If it is hard for you to see if your body is really lined up as in the drawing, ask someone else to check you. Start with your head. Pull it up tall and stretch it. Then check the rest of your body, to see if it is in line with the string.

Once you have your body lined up in a tall, poised stance, you are ready to learn to walk gracefully. It helps to have someone check out your walk, because many people have developed bad walking habits, of which they are not even aware. Your walk may demonstrate self-consciousness, shyness, fear, carelessness or a manner of being too forward. Instead, you want your walk to speak of grace and ease.

There is a lovely way to sit, too, though it is not done often enough. Many times an attractive girl spoils the whole effect of her beauty by sitting with her lower limbs wrapped around the chair legs, or twisted into awkward pretzel shapes under the chair. Or there are those who don't keep their skirts down.

Above are two correct sitting positions that you should practice:

1. The best position (left) is to sit with your ankles crossed. Bring them over to the side of the leg which is in front. Hold your knees tightly together and point your feet to the side.

2. *If you must cross your legs,* cross them at the knees (right), then pull both legs to the side. Keep your ankles closely together and point your toes down. Tuck your skirt closely to your knees. Warning: Crossing your legs at the knees *incorrectly* can cause varicose veins and cut off the circulation in your legs. It also destroys poise.

Practice standing and sitting correctly until these ways become natural to you. Practice much at home, to look relaxed and at ease in public.

A student wrote: "Last week I had to represent my company at an informal court hearing. Two months ago I would have fallen apart before I got to the witness stand. Instead, I felt confident, since I knew I was walking and sitting properly. This was my first real test since we had class. It's hard for me to describe my feeling, since it was so new and unfamiliar. But it was a *good* feeling.''

Yes, body language is a wonderful tool for self-improvement. It will help you feel better about yourself and look more attractive, too. But it's not just something that will happen because you have read this book. Practice makes perfect!

Assignment: Body Language

1. Ask someone to check out your posture as you line up your body against the string on the mirror, as was suggested in this chapter.

2. When you are at home alone, practice sitting properly in front of a mirror. Practice facial expressions that you would use if you were listening to a speaker (such as blinking your eyes and looking directly at the speaker and smiling) until it *looks natural*. The next time you are attending a meeting, remember to do all these things.

3. Think of five ways in which you might respond *with enthusiasm* to an invitation. Write them down. Practice saying them out loud.

4. Write down five ways in which you might invite, with enthusiasm, someone else to do something with you. Practice saying them out loud.

Part IV

Weight Control

For instance, take the matter of eating. God has given us an appetite for food and stomachs to digest it. But that doesn't mean we should eat more than we need. Don't think of eating as important, because some day God will do away with both stomachs and food.

1 Corinthians 6:13

9

Minimizing the Maximums

Three years ago a twenty-six-year-old friend of mine was a slender bride. Now she was suddenly a huge blimp of a woman, fully over a hundred pounds overweight. Her husband was disgusted. She was depressed. But she couldn't seem to keep from stuffing herself with junk food.

One night her husband sat watching her wolf down her food at the supper table. He frowned. "You know, Barbara, if you don't lose some weight, I'm going to divorce you," he said. Then he laughed, to show that he was teasing. But Barbara couldn't forget the look in his eye. Her husband couldn't stand the sight of her puffy, misshapen body. What could she do?

"I'll start dieting again," she told herself. Then she ran back to her bedroom, where she had hidden a bag full of chocolate kisses. She ate them all that evening.

Barbara came to my classes. She began to see herself as made in the image of God. She began to realize that since God loved her, He would help her with her compulsion to overeat. She also began to gain some insight into the reasons why she could not stick to a diet. She had been in a terrible depression ever since her baby had been born dead. Intellectually she knew that this tragedy was not her fault, but she could not help feeling that it was a reflection on her worth as a person. Life was out to get her. She would soothe her pain with food.

Realizing that she needed to learn to accept herself, Barbara began going to a church psychologist. After many hours of counseling and soul searching, she lost sixty pounds and gained a happier husband and a better outlook on life.

Many large women tell me that they consume fewer calories than slender people, and yet they gain. What they say may be true, for there can be physical reasons for putting on pounds that have nothing to do with the amount of food that is eaten. A trip to the doctor will determine whether the reason is physical or psychological. In fact, any serious weight-loss program should include a physical checkup before you begin.

When Karen entered my class, she readily admitted she needed to lose seventy-nine pounds. "But I hardly eat anything at all. I don't understand how I gain," she insisted.

I wondered if the reason might not be psychological; but I knew that if it were, she would not be able to admit it to me—or even to herself. So, I just asked, "Have you had a good physical?"

"Yes, and there's nothing wrong with me," she insisted. I didn't try to argue with her, but encouraged her to continue the classes. Soon she began to lose. Several months later, she had lost all but eleven of the seventy-nine excess pounds. She wrote me a letter to tell me all about how it had happened.

"I felt like the class you taught was a neat-sounding thing. Yet, I went into it determined not to let myself like you. I had such a chip on my shoulder, a resentment toward anyone who was a gracious, confident, attractive person. I really felt awful, and I know now I looked it, too. But God had other plans for me. I just thank Him so much for bringing about the change in me . . . . My attitudes are different now, my outlook on life is different, and I love it."

She went on to admit that "a typical day in my life last fall might have included staying in bed as late as I possibly could, eating from the time I got up until I went to bed, resting and watching TV, as I was always tired, or going to town for lunch, which was always fattening and expensive.

"Today, the first day that all three of my children were in school at once, I got out my bike, rode three miles, had coffee (black) with a neighbor, came home, vacuumed, burned the trash, fixed lunch for my son and myself, wrote a letter, ran to town to the library and grocery store, came home and now I am washing clothes and writing to you! My days are full and beautiful—I have a new life!"

Karen said that when she was fat, she sometimes dropped in at her husband's office at noon, but never received an invitation to go to lunch. Now that she is slender, her husband admits that he used to make up excuses why he could not eat away from the office on those days. He had simply been ashamed to be seen with his fat wife.

Karen now marvels that she had been carrying around on her body over sixty extra pounds—about the same amount that her eleven-year-old daughter weighs. Little wonder she had no energy for doing anything! *The amazing part is that she could blot out the fact that she was overeating.* Being fat sometimes makes us so sensitive to criticism, so defensive, that we cannot admit our responsibility for our condition, even to ourselves.

How many brides do you know who say their marriage vows and retire from all supervision of their minds and bodies at the same time? How many wives in their mid-thirties do you know who are completely incompatible with their husbands, both physically and socially?

And how many successful, well-groomed businessmen, married to such wives, work more hours than they need at the office because they do not want to see their wives' sloppy appearance and blithe acceptance of everything they have provided?

Many of these wives think of themselves as good Christians, but they are only fooling themselves, as Anita Bryant and Bob Green point out so well in their book *Running the Good Race:* "At churches all over the country we see great Christian ladies who don't smoke, don't drink, don't wear cosmetics—you name it, they don't do it—but they are obese.

"They may go out and knock on doors, witness, and do everything good Christians are supposed to do, but what kind of example do they set? In effect they are saying to the non-Christian, 'Hey, look at me. I'm following the rules and regulations of Christian behavior to the letter. I wouldn't drink, wear makeup, dance, or do any of those numbers, but I do weigh two hundred pounds.' It's ridiculous."

Let's look at what the Bible says about our bodies: "Know ye not that ye are the temple of God . . . ?" (1 Corinthians 3:16 KJV). Have you neglected God's creation, or made it unrecognizable?

Paul said, ". . . Your own body does not belong to you. For God has bought you with a great price. So use every part of your body to give glory back to God, because he owns it" (1 Corinthians 6:19, 20).

One way of glorifying God, then, is by keeping our bodies clean, neat and in good condition. But the Bible goes even further in warning against overeating. "For instance, take the matter of eating. God has given us an appetite for food and stomachs to digest it. But that doesn't mean we should eat more than we need . . ." (1 Corinthians 6:13). Ouch, that hurts!

Running the Good Race also points out that once a person weighs thirty percent more than the standards set by insurance companies, the risk of all diseases—including cancer and accidents—increases. "The fact is," says Bob Green, "it's a sin the way most Americans eat!"

Not only my appearance suffers with a weight gain; my personality does, too. When I overeat, I become lazy. Therefore I am less effective in everything I do, and I take out my frustration on others—even my dear family!

The same hostility is apt to develop in those who have been on a diet and then fall away. Do I tell my children and husband that I am really angry at myself because I have overeaten? It's easier to be cross and start nagging than to admit my problem.

I have had to go through the painful process of dieting again and again. I figure that over the years I've lost as much as 3,000 pounds. So surely my words must hold some weight!

Seriously, I want you to know that I don't regret the discipline that has been learned in saying no to some foods that are not good for me. It makes it easier to say no to other temptations. Therefore, every part of my life runs smoother.

You, also, can see the positive side of dieting, as God can truly turn our physical weaknesses into moral strengths. It takes a big person (mentally, not physically) to acknowledge that there is a real problem. Sometimes the truth hurts. I hope that you will resolve today to become all that you can be.

". . . Anything is possible if you have faith" (Mark 9:23).

10

The Fat Heart

Lena Westmark, in an article titled "Fat Christians on the Narrow Way" (*Light and Life Magazine*), points out that to lose weight, we must follow a spiritual path.

She urged her readers to think of overeating as a spiritual concern, even a sin; because sin exists where you, in spite of your good intentions, refuse to accept responsibility and exercise self-control.

"Somehow it's impossible to see Christ as overweight. Can you imagine His followers' reactions if Christ would have folded His hands over a fat paunch when He said, 'If any man will come after me, let him deny himself'?" she wrote.

Fatness is not, then, the sign of a person who likes himself. It is instead the measurement of the sickness of the soul which is encased in it. Proverbs 15:32 says it so well: "He who neglects discipline despises himself" (NAS)—and gains more weight.

If you can admit that you have a problem, you are taking the first step toward becoming slim. God had a special shape for you when He made you. By opening yourself to His will for you, you can attain it. As with all life's problems, fighting fat can take you on an exciting spiritual journey, in which you also learn to develop inner character. Like the reformed alcoholic who knows he cannot ever sip one drop of wine, you may need to learn to forswear even a spoonful of a chocolate sundae for the rest of your life. You have the opportunity to learn such discipline that will perhaps inspire a fellow struggler.

"No temptation has come your way that is too hard for flesh and blood to bear. But God can be trusted not to allow you to suffer any temptation beyond your powers of endurance. He will see to it that every temptation has its way out, so that it will be possible for you to bear it" (1 Corinthians 10:13 PHILLIPS).

If you have been stuffing your spiritual vacuum with food, you will be pleasantly surprised at the deeper satisfaction you gain by filling it with Jesus Christ. Communicate with God. He will listen to you and strengthen you to stay on a good diet. As you lose pounds, your soul will feast on God.

How do you choose a good diet out of the bewildering and often conflicting array available today? I don't believe there is any one diet that is magical enough to shed pounds from all of us. The diet that works for you could very well be injurious to your neighbor's health! For instance, the high-protein/high-fat diet may cause some to lose, but increase cholesterol to levels that would be harmful to those with cardiovascular problems. A vegetarian diet may help alleviate the world protein shortage, but the heavy reliance on calorie-laden soybeans and health-food bread may add, rather than subtract, pounds.

Simply try cutting out the rich, gooey desserts when you find the pounds creeping up, along with the French fries, pizza and pasta. And order a scoop (no more) of cottage cheese and cantaloupe for lunch instead of a cheeseburger, and drink your coffee black. For dinner you have four ounces of meat or poultry, with all visible fat removed, and a couple of vegetables. Make sure to include, every day, something from each of the four food groups: fish, meat, poultry, eggs; milk and dairy products; fruits and vegetables; breads and cereals. This kind of diet is safe and works for most people who have no special health problems.

Remember, always consult a doctor before starting a diet—and ask God's help daily, so you can stick to it. "A man without self-control is as defenseless as a city with broken-down walls" (Proverbs 25:28). Select a good diet and stay on it.

Basic good health rules are important for everyone. For instance, constipation is a real detriment to good health. Yet, in most cases, it can be overcome by consuming six to eight glasses of water each day. Drinking enough water not only helps eliminate the wastes from your body, but it also is a marvelous way to clear up a bad complexion.

The ideal way to start the morning is to take two glasses of warm water. I have to admit that sixteen ounces of tepid water makes me gag, and I don't get it down every morning! Sometimes the size of my glass gets pretty small! But make sixteen ounces your goal, at any rate. Squeeze one-third to one-half of a fresh lemon into the water, in order to help purify your system. Be sure to use real lemon juice, then brush your teeth to remove the acid, which could destroy tooth enamel.

Soon your body will be in the habit of accomplishing a regular bowel movement every morning. If the water does not produce a regular elimination, try buying bran at a health food store. Take one to two tablespoons with each meal.

If you are overweight, you should eliminate all fat-producing starches and sugars from your diet. Make sure you eat lots of vegetables, salads and proteins. Eat fruits in moderate amounts.

Many people feel they should be able to lose weight if they hold their daily intake of calories to a certain level. But doctors at Brookhaven National Laboratory have proved that a calorie of sugar adds two to five times more blood fat than does a calorie of starch. Counting calories is not enough. You might be able to eat small quantities of breads, potatoes and spaghetti, but if you eat the same amount of cake, watch out!

11

The Way of the Will

When I decided the time had come for me to lose thirty pounds, I started dieting on December 23, just as I bought the Christmas turkey! Friends thought I was crazy! They urged me to stuff for Christmas and diet for the New Year. But I knew that if I ate my way through all that holiday fudge and fruitcake, I would have that many more pounds to take off. I kept reminding myself how much easier it was to gain than to lose. I did get rid of those extra pounds. Now I look and feel so much better!

Some of my friends looked at the new, sleek me and said, "That's okay for you, but I haven't got any willpower. When I'm eating out and everyone else orders pie a la mode, I want some, too."

How do you gain enough self-discipline to eat what you must, rather than what you desire? I suggest that you use every trick in this book! Keep track of all the calories you have resisted in ordering a salad instead of the pie a la mode, and write the number down in a notebook you carry with you just for that purpose. You will not only be giving yourself credit for having resisted temptation; but you'll be reminding yourself of the danger of calories. Anyway, as you write the figure down, you can indulge in a smugly noble feeling that is almost as rewarding as the taste of cherry pie with ice cream.

Another way to build the muscles of your willpower is to tie a bell on your refrigerator door! If you attempt to snack between meals, it rings like a burglar alarm. Or paste a color photo of a beautiful girl in a bikini to the inside of your refrigerator door. Every time you open it, you can remind yourself you want to look just like that. Chances are you will shut the door without eating anything. This trick backfired for one of my students, however. She found her husband wanting to peek at the beautiful girl on the refrigerator door so often that the food inside was becoming far too warm!

Another one of my students had a photo of herself at her heaviest enlarged to poster size, then put it on the refrigerator door. It was a good reminder of what she *didn't* want to look like. If you want to heighten the effect, have a photo of yourself made in a bikini. It's guaranteed to keep the refrigerator door closed.

If snacking while you cook for the family is your downfall, a doctor suggested this: Try placing a can of low-calorie drink on the counter as you work. When the urge to taste the goodies you are making hits you, take a sip of the diet drink instead.

My pastor was told by his doctor not to eat a thing unless he was seated at the dinner table. That meant he couldn't walk through the kitchen and take a cracker from the cupboard unless he sat at the table to eat it. He couldn't snack on ice cream between TV commercials unless he sat down in the dining room. What excellent advice! If every time we took a bonbon from the candy dish we had to walk to the dining room table and sit down to eat it, we probably wouldn't bother.

Practice eating slowly. After taking a bite of food, lay the fork down, chew the food and swallow. Only then should you take up the fork for another bite. You'll eat less. Practice sipping your drinks slowly, too. Enjoy the mood you have created. If you spend as much time eating as the others do at the table, you scarcely notice the difference in amount.

To fool your eyes, always fill your plate—even if with only some glamorous (and low calorie) carrot curls and garnishes. Learn *not* to be a plate cleaner. The food you leave on your plate is just that much that won't go to fat.

Keep track of your progress by making a weight chart on graph paper and tack it on the bedroom wall as a constant reminder. Begin with your present weight and record it every day. On the first day, weigh right after your dinner. From then on, get on the scales the first thing in the morning, when you normally weigh the least. The immediate loss you achieve from dinner to breakfast the next morning will give you a nice psychological starting boost, rather like a swimmer who is allowed to push off from the side of the pool during a meet.

Set goals for each week. Mark your weekly weight loss in red. Every time you have lost five or ten pounds, give yourself a reward—a new pair of earrings, a ticket to a movie, or some other nonfattening treat. Read some of the readily available books on weight control, or join a weight-losing group.

Proteins, Preservatives and Perseverance

Whether we are fat or thin, we all need to learn more about nutrition. Science tells us that our bodies rebuild themselves every seven years. If you begin today to put into your body the foods containing the correct nutrition, you will have a whole new you within seven years! That new creature is going to look a lot more glamorous if you eliminate refined sugar, French fries and cake. Concentrate on good proteins and salads. You will feel better, too.

Today most of our organs have to fight to utilize or eliminate such adulterated foods as cola drinks, sugared cereals, white flour, white sugar, instant packaged foods and other highly refined products. Preservatives and chemicals work further destruction. We are like cars designed only to run on unleaded gas, into which we have poured leaded fuel. Our insides get all fouled up.

The Scripture says in Isaiah 55:2, "Why spend your money on foodstuffs that don't give you strength? Why pay for groceries that don't do you any good? . . ." Although this passage is referring to spiritual food, I feel the same advice can be applied to our physical life.

Nutrition is a very involved study, and many good books have been written specifically on nutrition. We need to read them, for most doctors receive very little training on nutrition in medical school. Consequently, most cure illnesses, rather than prevent sickness. If you prefer to be disease free, rather than ailing and under a doctor's care, study nutrition. This could be your solution.

An old New England joke has a waiter inquiring of a diner, "And how did you find the steak this evening?" The patron replies, "I picked up one of the peas and there it was." I hope the diner was not dieting. Meats like steak, chops and roast beef are high-protein foods. These help dieters shed fat faster than the high-carbohydrate peas.

Actually, both the peas and the meat happen to have the same amount of calories. But when you eat the higher-quality protein of meat, you increase your metabolic rate. In other words, your body burns up protein calories faster than carbohydrate calories. When calories are burned, they are not stored as fat in your body.

Other good proteins are fish, poultry and eggs. High carbohydrate foods which you should restrict are corn, white or sweet potatoes, fresh lima beans and, of course, the fresh peas that our New England diner ate.

Once you've learned about nutrition, you can make good use of the labels on cans and packaged foods when you shop, The ingredients listed first on the label make up the largest percentage of the contents. When you buy a can of beef stew, for instance, you can tell whether you're getting more potatoes (carbohydrates) than beef (proteins) by noting which is listed first on the label. If the beef is the ingredient that is listed last, coming after water and spices, you can be sure you're getting very little protein! Labels also must list the preservatives and chemicals used in the finished product.

So learn to eat right nutritionally, and practice self-discipline in controlling the amounts you eat. You will begin to look and feel better right away.

12

Hooray for Exercise

My husband called me from town one day to ask if I needed anything from the grocery store. "We have plenty of food," I said, then added, "What I really need is some jogging shoes." There was a long silence from Jim. After all, he has always been the athletic one in our family. While he had excelled in almost every sport, all I ever did was watch.

The remark about jogging shoes popped out of my mouth because of a nagging realization that I needed the exercise. When we are in our teens or twenties, exercise is desirable. But when we are in our thirties, it is the only way to keep our figures. And by the time we are in our forties and fifties, we must exercise or fall apart!

So when I joked about jogging shoes, Jim took me seriously. He couldn't react fast enough. He went by the sporting goods store and bought jogging shoes, socks, shorts and a shirt for me. "Quick!" he told the clerk. "Wrap them up before my wife changes her mind." My little jest was to turn into a whole new way of life for Jim and me!

At first I hated jogging. It was very hard work. I could jog only a few blocks before collapsing on a curb to catch my breath. But gradually I jogged additional blocks. And finally I was jogging all the way to the Dairy Queen where my son was working—a trip of three and a half miles. (He never even let me have a "snack"!)

Most people like to jog in the early morning, but for me the best time is about eleven at night, after the classes are finished. Jim always goes with me for protection, as we feel it is unsafe to jog alone.

One night we jogged past a man who asked, "Do you have a light for my cigarette?"

"No, we don't," said Jim.

"I should have known you athletes didn't smoke," the man said. I can't tell you how wonderful his remark made me feel—even if I did realize that he was drunk! I, the perennial spectator, was being called an athlete!

"But you really are an athlete, now," Jim told me. "You're spitting cotton like a track star!" My mouth full of saliva was a sign that I had really become a genuine athlete!

Now I'm a confirmed jogger. Not only do I keep my weight under control by jogging; I feel wonderful. Running with Jim, laughing and working together (Oh, the dear Lord knows the work involved for me in jogging!) has been wonderful for our marriage. When there is no moon and I feel a bit afraid in the dark, I cling to Jim's arm. Because I have to speed up when he does, I make my best time with him. And jogging like this does wonders for romance. I think jogging helps a woman's sex life, too! I have to admit that sometimes I do feel grouchy about having to jog. I have to force myself to got out on the street. But within five minutes of jogging, I am happy as a lark. It has done wonders for us.

"Lazy people want much but get little, while the diligent are prospering" (Proverbs 13:4). Let's all be diligent and prosper by losing weight and gaining good health. "God delights in those who keep their promises . . ." (Proverbs 12:22).

I heard a man once say, "When I get the feeling that I need exercise, I lie down until the feeling goes away." How true that seems for most of us, but how very unfortunate if we do it!

If you are in doubt as to how much you should weigh, consult the desirable-weight chart on the next page, supplied by Metropolitan Life Insurance Company.

The ideal measurements also vary considerably according to

DESIRABLE WEIGHTS

Height in Shoes (One-inch Heels)	Small Frame	Medium Frame	Large Frame
4'10"	92–98	96–107	104–119
4'11"	94–101	98–110	106–122
5'0"	96–104	101–113	109–125
5'1"	99–107	104–116	117–128
5'2"	102–110	107–119	115–131
5'3"	105–113	110–122	118–134
5'4"	108–116	113–126	128–138
5'5"	111–119	116–130	125–142
5'6"	114–123	120–135	129–146
5'7"	118–127	124–139	133–150
5'8"	122–131	128–143	137–154
5'9"	126–135	132–147	141–158
5'10"	130–140	136–151	145–163
5'11"	134–144	140–155	149–168
6'0"	138–148	144–159	153–173

height and type of bone structure. As a rough guide, the bust and hips should measure the same. The waist should be about ten inches smaller.

For most of us, exercise is the miracle that enables us to lose inches as well as pounds. Not only does exercise tone the muscles, but it also encourages good posture and deep breathing. Always check with a doctor before beginning any kind of regular exercise program, to be sure that you have no serious health problem. But get started as soon as possible.

Almost all of us, no matter how old we are, can at least walk in the fresh air or do light gardening, such as growing potted plants. These are great ways to avoid the rather melancholy mood from which some of us suffer as we grow older. Let's get out of that rocking chair in front of the TV and move outside!

I think of Isaiah 58:11, which says, "And the Lord will guide you continually, and satisfy you with all good things, and keep you healthy, too; and you will be like a well-watered garden, like an ever-flowing spring." I want this in my life. Don't you?

Mildred Cooper and Kenneth H. Cooper, M.D., in their excellent book, *Aerobics for Women,* tell us that aerobic exercises will help us liberate our bodies, look better, feel better and live our lives more fully. Aerobic exercises increase the amount of oxygen your body can utilize, and then deliver it to every nook and cranny of the body where food is stored. Once you are aerobically conditioned, you can produce energy in abundance, lose weight and reduce heart and blood pressure problems.

Younger women who practice aerobics will look and feel better. They will have fewer complications with menstruation and pregnancy. Older women will keep their youthful-looking tissues. Their legs and skin will be prettier. Some avoid menopausal problems.

In order to exercise aerobically, you must use your body so strenuously that you make your heart beat 130 to 150 times per minute for a sustained period. (These are rates for women.) You may jog, walk, skip rope, climb stairs, swim or bicycle. Each activity requires various amounts of time to reach the levels required to make your heart work hard.

I used to think I could not do such strenuous exercise, because I have a bad back. However, when my doctor gave me permission, I began to jump rope, and later (thanks to my husband!) to jog. I'm also learning racket-ball, so that I can exercise when the weather outside is rainy, as it often is in the winter in Oregon.

If you are interested in a calorie-burning exercise, buy a standard jump rope from a sporting goods store, or use sash cord in sizes seven to ten. The rope should be long enough to reach from armpit to armpit while passing under the feet. As with jogging, work up *gradually* to the level that is best for your age. You might want to check with a physical-education instructor about the best procedure. Of course, clear any exercise routine through your doctor.

There are two important safety rules to observe about jumping rope. Never participate in this exercise barefooted, and always be sure to jump on a carpeted surface or grass. When I first started jumping rope, I found that my rope was hitting the ceiling, so I went outside, on the concrete patio. Since I couldn't find my tennis shoes at the moment, I kicked off the shoes I was wearing and began to jump barefooted. I completely overlooked the safety rules. Sure enough, I badly bruised my toes. The pain reminded me of my carelessness for a long time!

Without eating a single calorie less than you usually do, you can take twenty-five pounds off each year, simply by adding thirty minutes of exercise to your daily routine. Here are some special exercises that can help you to lose inches in the proper places:

Bustline and posture—Stretch out flat on your stomach with your legs together and your toes pointed. Bend your arms at right angles, place your hands with the palms flat on the floor and the fingers pointed in. Begin to raise your body, pushing with arm and chest muscles. Do not bend your knees. When your arms are completely extended, lower your body in easy stages. Hold your tummy in throughout the exercise. Repeat ten times.

Waist—Lie with your back on the floor with your legs straight in front of you. Hold your arms outstretched. Sit up and raise your left leg at the same time, touching your right elbow to your left knee. Return to the starting position with arms outstretched, legs together and with the toes pointed slightly. Your knees should be straight. Sit up again and turn your body in the opposite direction, raising your right leg and touching your right knee with your left elbow.

Abdomen—Lie on your back with your arms extended above your head and your legs raised and bent at the knees. Sit up, bringing your arms parallel with your legs, and try to hold this position for a few seconds. Raise your arms and hold them for a few seconds, then roll back to the floor.

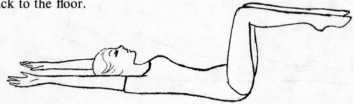

Hips—Start by lying flat on your stomach with your toes pointed and your chin rested on folded arms. Move your legs apart sideways about a foot and a half, with your toes pointed and knees held straight. Lift your legs several inches above the floor and hold them in the air for a few seconds. Bring your legs together in the air and hold that position for a few seconds. Then lower your legs slowly.

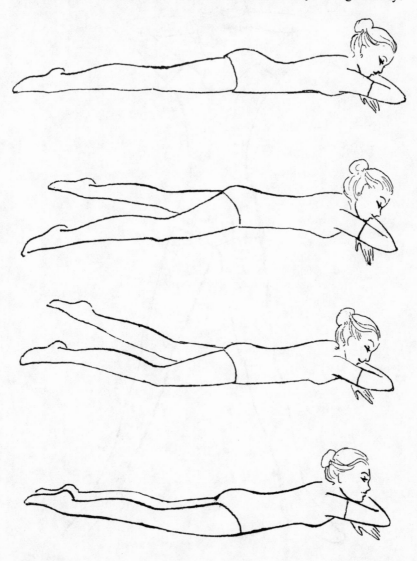

Thighs—Stand with your legs apart and your feet pointed outward. Your hands should be clasped behind your head, your elbows up. Put your weight on the right leg, bend your right knee and extend your left leg. Resume the standing position and change directions.

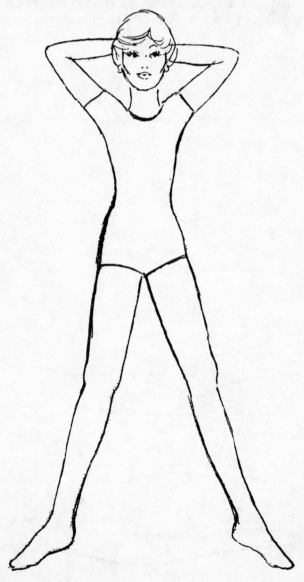

Many sports also trim inches off the body. To reduce the midriff and waist and tighten your abdominal muscles, try tennis, badminton, golf, softball, rowing, canoeing, fly-casting, volleyball and basketball. To trim hips and legs, do skiing, ice-skating, roller skating, fencing, bowling, bicycling, mountain climbing, touch football, surfing, hiking and water skiing.

Here are some tips for getting the most out of your daily exercise routines. Try to do them at the same time every day. If you're not in the mood, turn on the stereo or the radio for appropriate background music. Try to exercise right before you eat a meal. You will have less desire to eat, if you do. If you eat correctly, use your willpower, ask God to help you with your weight problem and exercise, you are going to look wonderful!

Assignment: Weight Control

1. See your doctor for a good physical checkup.

2. Check your weight against the chart in this chapter to see if you are above the maximum for your height and bone structure. If you are, count the number of calories you eat every day for a week.

3. Read at least one good book on nutrition.

4. Choose the exercises or sports that most appeal to you, and plan a time in your day when you can do them.

5. Keep a weight chart as described in this chapter. Ask God to give you the willpower to diet. He wants to help you lose weight. He will help you, if you let Him!

Part V

Hair Care

King Solomon: ". . . . What a lovely filly you are, my love! How lovely your cheeks are, with your hair falling down upon them! How stately your neck with that long string of jewels. We shall make you golden earrings and silver beads."

Song of Solomon 1:9–11

13

Exterior Decorating

Have you ever been watching a shampoo commercial on TV with your husband when suddenly four or five models with long, richly colored hair begin tossing their tresses at the camera? Did you ever see that man you married lean forward to stare at those gleaming locks, as if hypnotized?

And did you ever have the urge to throw something at the TV when the announcer said you could have hair just like those beautiful girls, simply by using the shampoo he is selling? There is more to having beautiful hair than just choosing the right kind of suds. First you must have healthy hair. It must be styled right for your face. You have to know how to condition, and to roll, blow dry or back comb if you want pretty hair.

If you are like most of us, you didn't throw something at the TV. You just told yourself you didn't have the time nor the money for all that foolishness. You decided to let your hair grow as it would, brush it one hundred times a night and be done with it.

But, if that's what you did, I hope you will reconsider. After all, no matter where a man works these days, he is likely to be surrounded by beautiful women—females who spend a lot on their hair, to make it every bit as glamorous as those models in the shampoo commercials. It's no treat for your husband to come home and see you with your hair straggling out of a messy ponytail or hanging in mop strings.

In many cases, I think women don't know what to do with their hair. So they take refuge in 1 Peter 3:3, 4 (PHILLIPS), which says, "Your beauty should not be dependent on an elaborate coiffure, or on the wearing of jewellery or fine clothes, but on the inner personality—the unfading loveliness of a calm and gentle spirit, a thing very precious in the eyes of God."

I know women who claim that this verse is a commandment that forbids them to improve the appearance of their hair. But this Scripture says that your beauty should not be *dependent* on these external things. There is a big difference.

If you have read the earlier chapters of this book, you are probably already working hard to become inwardly beautiful, for you recognize that inner beauty and personality contribute the highest percentage to your total beauty quotient. You will remember that in our recipe for loveliness, other important ingredients were good posture and positive body language. Only a small percent of the ingredients consisted of the exterior decoration which can be achieved with good grooming.

In this section on hair care and the next on cosmetics, we are going to work on that last percent. If you think it should not be necessary to put so much effort into something that counts so little, remember that people naturally gravitate to the object that is pleasing to the senses. If something looks, feels and smells good, we like it. Our hair and our skin can be the lovely frame for the artistic masterpiece that pleases the eye, the subtle chord in the melody that tantalizes the ear, the dash of cinnamon in the apple pie that draws us to the kitchen.

It is not impossible for you to have beautiful hair. Believe it, even if you feel that what is now on your head more nearly resembles broomstraws than the spun gold of fairy tales.

Getting the Gleam

Let's start at the beginning. What is it that makes hair beautiful? I would like to give credit to my hair-care teacher, Harvey Loveall, for consultation regarding this chapter.

The physical condition of your whole body, as well as your emotions, will affect the appearance of your hair. If you don't get enough sleep or exercise . . . if you fail to consider nutrition in your diet . . . even if you smoke or drink . . . your hair will likely be dull and dry. Even if you are simply worried or depressed, you may find your hair lacks luster. These emotions impair the circulation to your scalp.

If you could peer through an electron microscope at a single hair, you would see that it is covered with tiny scale-like layers, which circle the hair shaft. Underneath the top layer are many other layers. In shiny hair, all of these scales are lying down parallel to the hair shaft, producing a smooth surface, which reflects light. In dull hair, the scales are swollen up so that they are peeled back from the shaft. There is no way a hair shaft covered with prickly scales can reflect light.

If you want healthy hair, with every scale lying down, you should eat plenty of meats, eggs, fish, cottage cheese, seeds and nuts. Why? Hair is 98 percent protein, and these natural foods are high in protein.

Be sure that your body has sufficient Vitamin A (available in whole milk, cod-liver oil, liver, kidney, sweetbreads, butter, cream and egg yolk). It is a necessity not only for healthy hair, but for good skin, teeth and vision as well. A flaky skin and scalp may indicate a deficiency of Vitamin A. But don't overdose. Too much Vitamin A could cause peeling skin, loss of hair, headaches and even loss of eyesight, because the body cannot excrete the excess as it does with other vitamins. If you begin taking Vitamin A, use it for two or three months and compare results.

Taking Vitamin E (available naturally in nuts, fresh wheat germ, and stone-ground whole wheat cereal and bread) also can make your hair healthier, because it helps to keep Vitamin A from being oxidized and lost to your body. Both Vitamins A and B6 (available naturally in yeast, blackstrap molasses, wheat bran and germ, liver, heart and kidney) help the skin and hair retain the moisture which makes them pliable.

Many people have dull hair because they are using the wrong kind of shampoos, conditioners, creme rinses, coloring agents and permanent wave solutions. The price you pay for these products may have nothing to do with how good they are. If you use highly alkaline hair products, the scales of each hair shaft will swell. Your hair could become as dull and dry as burlap. If you use a product that is too acid, your hair will become brittle. The ideal hair product should be within the 4.5 to 5.6 pH range (alkaline/acid balance). Anything above this rating will make your hair dry and lifeless. Even water, rated at seven, and considered neutral, is too alkaline for the hair. But don't use anything rated below 4.5. Such a product could be dangerous to your hair. You may also rate your own shampoos, rinses and conditioners by buying a pH testing kit from the drugstore. All you have to do is dip a piece of the litmus paper from the kit into the product you want to test. Compare the color that the paper turns with a chart on the box that tells you exactly how alkaline the product is. Don't touch the paper with your fingers, or the reading may be inaccurate.

The Big Brush-Off

Do you brush your hair one hundred times a night? If so, you are wasting your time. That old wives' beauty rule should have been abolished from the boudoir about the time that scrub boards were retired from home laundries. The hair-brushing routine never really did anything to make your hair healthier. It simply distributed the oil produced at the scalp more evenly over the hair and cleansed dust and dirt that collected during the day out of the hair. Since women nowadays shampoo their hair more frequently than in your grandmother's day, prolonged brushing is no longer necessary. (But always brush your hair vigorously before washing it.)

What about dandruff? While almost all women believe they have dandruff, few do. The actual disease of dandruff is caused by an infection and results in rough, red, painful areas on the scalp. What most people experience is the natural flaking off of the dead cells of the scalp, often caused by harsh products. The same sloughing off of dead cells goes on constantly all over our bodies.

You can minimize flaking by shampooing your hair frequently with a good, balanced shampoo containing conditioners (not creme rinses). Many manufacturers produce shampoos with formulas both for oily or dry hair. Have a professional help you choose the one that is prepared especially for your type of hair. If you need to wash your hair every day to reduce the flaking, go ahead. Frequent shampooing won't damage your hair in any way if you use a pH-balanced conditioning product.

Remember that flaking will be worse if you use a hair spray that contains a lot of alcohol, which dries your hair. Lacquer-based hair sprays immediately seal the skin pores and can cause one's scalp to itch and become scaly.

Never use a super-hold spray. The best sprays are made of all-natural, organic substances. Look for a spray labeled, "No lacquer, water soluble." And when you're spraying, remember to hold the container at exactly the distance the label recommends. In view of recent warnings, try to use non-aerosol products.

If your hair has become lifeless through too much exposure to the sun or to a bad hair product, you will want to use a hair conditioner. When you have found a conditioner with a 4.5 to 5.5 pH rating, work it into your hair. Put a plastic bag around your hair and sit under a dryer for ten to fifteen minutes. If you don't have a dryer, leave the conditioner on your hair and keep it covered with the bag for at least twenty minutes. You may safely keep it that way and sleep on it overnight, if you wish. A conditioner cannot do any harm if left on your hair a long time. Also, it cannot do any permanent good if you leave it on your hair only two to three minutes.

A creme rinse will make your hair become more slippery and easier to comb, but it will not make any permanent change in your hair's condition. Use a conditioner, not a creme rinse, for problem hair. Some creme rinses contain the same ingredients as floor wax does, in order to make hair shine. This ingredient builds up, just like floor wax, to give your hair a plastic, greasy look. Then it must be removed.

Once you have learned how to keep your hair healthy, you will be ready for the exciting business of styling your hair. Some women who come to The Image of Loveliness courses have been wearing the same hairstyle as grandmothers that they wore as brides. "My husband likes it this way, and I'm afraid to change," they usually explain.

Yes, sometimes it is difficult to adjust to a different hairstyle after thirty years. But even husbands can get used to the new you. It's like remodeling the kitchen. The family may miss the old breakfast nook, but the pleasure of having room for a new washer, dryer and freezer in the kitchen makes everyone appreciate that sleek new serving bar that took its place. Before long, everyone remembers that the old nook was too dark, anyway. As you read the next chapter on hair styling, do keep an open mind. It's wonderful how women can improve their appearance by choosing a different hairstyle. Consider a new look for yourself!

14

Getting the Most From Your Stylist

While many women successfully do all their hair care entirely by themselves, most of us should go to a beauty salon for three procedures—haircuts, hair coloring and permanent waves. Only if you have what is known as an average head of hair will you be able to use these products without possibly damaging your hair. Remember that every snowflake is created with a unique structure. The very hairs of your head are not only numbered by God (Matthew 10:30); they are composed of an entirely different texture from your neighbor's.

The product that makes your hair as limp as cooked spaghetti may make your best friend's as brittle and flighty as an electrified wire. The coloring that turns your hair a rich chestnut brown might make hers look green, purple or scorched-pan black.

Often women who try to give themselves permanents or color their own hair end up with a coiffure that resembles a sponge. They eventually spend more time and money repairing the damage done than if they had used professionals in the first place. The problem is that they simply do not know how to use the additives that compensate for the differences in types of hair.

Besides, you can learn a lot from your cosmetologist that will definitely make a trip to the salon now and then worthwhile. You should not have to be a regular customer to get his advice, either. A lot of women feel their stylists will be unhappy if they come to the salon only once a month for a haircut or coloring job. But that is not true. I used to go weekly to have my hair done, but now I go once about every five weeks for a trim. I have learned to care for my own hair in between times, because I was taught how to do it by my wonderful hairdresser!

Perhaps you don't have a hairdresser, and you're ready to make a complete change in hairstyle or color, or you need a permanent wave or a haircut. If you want to get the most for your money, choose your stylist carefully. On your first visit, don't request any drastic change. Don't walk in off the street and ask to go platinum blonde or have your waist-length hair sheared off. On the first visit, just have a shampoo and set. Talk about your ultimate goals and listen to his suggestions.

Communicate with your hairdresser. Let him know there's a voice under that hair. If you don't know exactly what you want, tell him what you do not want. Also, tell him about all the little peculiarities of your hair, such as the fact that it won't hold a set, or that it flies every which way. Consider his suggestions. If you still like them by the time you come in the next week, go ahead and take the plunge. By then you will know if the hairdresser is willing to spend individual time with you, and you can be reassured that you won't end up looking like the five ladies who left just before you came in!

Your very best investment at the beauty shop is a good haircut. Trying to have beautiful hair without the proper cut is like trying to build a house without a foundation. With a good haircut, many women are able to do all the rest of their hair care by themselves and have a lovely coiffure.

Once you have a good haircut, be sure to keep it up. Since hair grows at the average rate of one-half inch per month, you should at least get a shaping every four to six weeks. You will be amazed at how your hair will respond with very little care.

How to Choose a New Hairstyle

In selecting a new hairstyle, it is essential to consider the shape of your face. Is it square, round, diamond shaped or pear shaped? If you are lucky, your face is a perfect oval. If it is any other shape, select a hairstyle in which the fullness of hair softens angular corners, too-strong jaws, receding chins or low foreheads.

Look into a mirror, holding your hair back so that only the face is showing. When you have determined your face shape, consider these hairstyling tips:

Square.   Use coiffures with the height arranged unevenly, especially if the silhouette tapers inward at the top. Don't arrange the hair too tightly on the forehead. Strive for a variety in the outline of the hair, such as a flip below the jawline.

WRONG   **RIGHT**

Heart shape. Coiffures that are widest below the temple are best. Don't pile your hair on your head. Let some hair soften the narrowness of the jaw. Bangs that fall below the hairline should form curved lines on the forehead.

WRONG   **RIGHT**

Oblong or long oval. Don't pile your hair on top of your head. A hairstyle that is widest in the middle of the head is best. Use a symmetrical coiffure without irregularities.

WRONG   **RIGHT**

Round.   Aim to lengthen, not shorten, the face. Avoid bangs that form a horizontal line across the forehead. A short haircut leaving the jawline free of hair might be good.

WRONG   **RIGHT**

Diamond shape.   Avoid any hairstyle which places fullness at the corners of the diamond. Hair should come down and fill out the jawline, and also be full at the top of the head.

WRONG   **RIGHT**

Pear shape. Don't let hair be loose and full around the jaw line and flat on top. Bring the hair loosely forward at temples, and add fullness to the top of the head.

WRONG	**RIGHT**

Oval shape. Do anything you want with your hair and rejoice! You can get by with it. However, older women will find that longer hair tends to add years.

Before you ask your stylist to give you a completely new look, you will also want to study magazine pictures that show *current* hairstyles. Cut out a few that you think would look good on you and show them to your hairdresser. Your stylist has years of experience in creating flattering hair arrangements. He may have solutions to your problems that you would never think of, and he will know if what you have selected will be suitable for you.

By all means, do discuss what you consider are your facial problems. Don't be afraid to tell him about the features of your face that you want to soften. If you think your nose is too big, tell him. Remember, others don't always notice what we consider a defect. If you don't mention that you think you have a big nose, he may not realize that you want to minimize it.

When you are discussing the pictures of hairstyles that you have brought with you, remember that not all of them may be practical for you because of your life-style, so explain your wishes to him.

Unless you have perfect hair, you can almost always improve it with a permanent wave. No longer do permanents come in one frizzy strength. Not all of them are even smelly! For every look that you could possibly want, there is a permanent created especially to achieve it. The reason that permanent waves should only be done in a salon is not that home products are bad. It is that each person's hair requires individual treatment. If your hair is dry, oily, limp, colored or tinted, the stylist will analyze the condition and add the necessary ingredients to give it full protection. If you have problems that will require additional minutes and different ingredients, you will require a more expensive permanent than someone who has average hair.

Making the choice to color your hair is not the weighty decision it once was. If you make a mistake, the stylist can tint your hair back to its original hue—or he can alter the new color.

Hair coloring should definitely be done by a professional, if you want the best results. Most people who color their hair at home end up with hair darker than they wanted. The color shown on the box will be true only if the chemical is added to perfectly white hair. On any other shade, even on very blonde hair, the color will be quite different.

If you should try to color your own hair and get into trouble, the best thing to do is phone your stylist for an appointment. Don't go around with purple hair for six months just because you made a mistake! One advantage of having your hair colored in a salon is that you can request many special effects, such as highlighting, which would be difficult to do at home. You will feel safer in asking for a complete change of color if your hairstylist does the work.

If you want to know how to roll your hair at home to achieve the look that your stylist achieves when he shampoos and sets your hair in the salon, ask him. He will probably tell you. A lot of do's and don'ts about making hair curl will be reviewed in the next chapter.

15

Creating Curls

What is the most effective way of putting curl into your hair? The best rollers to use are the smooth, plastic ones, often called magnetic rollers. If you try to use any roller that has prongs that catch and hold the hair, you will damage your hair. Sponge rollers don't provide enough tension to curl your hair. Snap-on rollers put two creases in each curl, which make for a messy comb-out. When you use magnetic rollers properly, the hair goes smoothly around them, leaving no stray wisps that will stick out at angles and dry that way.

To use magnetic rollers, first, be sure that your hair is absolutely wet. If it still doesn't stick, you may want to use a hair-setting solution, one that will not make your hair gummy. The solution should not be thick, gooey or flaky.

To place the rollers in your hair, take a section of hair no wider than the roller and comb it straight up. Then hold it at a 45-degree angle, off center. Place the roller and roll the hair down tightly, till the roller sits on its own base. By rolling tightly, you produce the tension that makes the hair curl. Fasten rollers with clips.

Another must in setting your hair is to be sure that it is absolutely dry before the comb-out. You will find that professional curling irons used in salons are always dry. They are usually hotter and work more effectively than the home appliances. But if you do buy a professional curling iron, be sure that you do not let it get so hot that it burns your hair. Test it this way: wrap a wet washcloth around the iron. If it steams and hisses, the iron is too hot. Always practice with a cold curling iron before attempting to use it while hot. There are many varieties of irons. Ask a professional for advice as to which would be best for your needs.

You may also find that electric rollers do not ordinarily produce a curl that will stay in your hair more than four or five hours. You just can't get the stretch and return of the hair that you do in a wet set.

The blow-dry method of curling your hair is popular today, but bear in mind that you must use a different technique than for the wet set. You can also use the blow-dry technique to *straighten* very curly hair.

Be sure to use a round brush when blow-drying your hair. Section off your hair and roll this brush into each section. You should draw the brush down, but not as tightly as if you were using a roller. Relax the tension somewhat as you dry each section. Just reverse the brush about a quarter of a turn, so that the hair is still around the brush, but not held tightly. As you blow into the section of hair, move the blower from side to side, so that too much heat is not concentrated at a single point.

If you want to straighten naturally curly hair, start the blow-dry process while your hair is wet. Stretch the hair out tight with the brush, without relaxing the tension. If you want to blow-dry curl into your hair, you may choose a brush that has fewer bristles and produces less grab, so that your hair will retain its elasticity. To straighten hair, use a brush with many bristles, so you can get a better grasp on your hair.

A *small amount* of back-combing is a good method of adding volume to hair. The object is to build a good cushion at the scalp *only*, leaving some hair to completely cover the cushion. However, a good permanent should eliminate the need for most back-combing. Be sure you do not end up with a bowling-ball look. Strive to achieve contour and softness, even though there is fullness. One of my students was told she should get rid of her World War II helmet! When she added some curl and softened the back-combing, she looked far more feminine and appealing!

Back-brushing is done in exactly the same way, except that a small brush is used. Back-brushing results in a much softer look than back-combing. To master these techniques, practice at home and ask your stylist's advice when you go in to see him. Once you have learned them, used the right products for your hair and visited your stylist for the important jobs, there is no reason whatsoever that you can't have soft and attractive hair.

Assignment: Hair Care

1. Study your face shape. Then cut current pictures from a magazine of hairstyles that would be suitable for you.

2. Go to the drugstore and buy a pH kit. Use it to test products you put into your hair.

3. Ask your stylist how you can set or curl your hair at home. Practice till you have the routine down perfectly.

Part VI

Skin Care

But we Christians have no veil over our faces; we can be mirrors that brightly reflect the glory of the Lord. And as the Spirit of the Lord works within us, we become more and more like him.
2 Corinthians 3:18

16

Skin Sins Can Be Forgiven

When someone looks into our faces, the first thing he sees is our skin. Either it glows healthily and attracts others, or it sags, wrinkles, flakes, breaks out and ruins our whole appearance.

Some of us think we can cure any kind of skin trouble with layers of makeup. But blemishes and dark spots will show through even the thickest foundation creams. Wrinkles, once they have arrived, will not disappear without plastic surgery.

Makeup can help an already-healthy skin look more lovely, but it is no substitute for a good complexion. In order to present a glowing face to the world, you must first concentrate on basic skin care programs that will prevent blemishes and wrinkles. Only then can you make the most of cosmetics.

If we are to reflect the Lord's glory and let Him make us more like Himself, we will want to present to others not just a clean face, but a radiant one, a face that attracts rather than repels.

In today's world, a poor complexion and pale cheeks and lips are ways of causing eyes to turn away from us. An unattractive skin, like a lighthouse with mud-splattered windows, keeps our inner radiance from shining through to those we want to help.

To look our best for God, we may want to shower, dress, comb our hair and apply color to our faces *before* we have our daily quiet time with Him. (But isn't it wonderful to know that He accepts us just the way we are—pin curls, sleepy eyes and all?)

If we know that we look our best, we will be ready to forget ourselves and use our lives in serving the Lord. We are going to look at some ways to improve our complexions in this chapter, so that we can look as lovely as possible.

Skin sins are real, and you may be causing many of them because you don't know what to do to avoid blemishes, dark spots, wrinkles and shiny noses. There is a way for these skin sins to be forgiven.

But, just as in our spiritual lives, the first step—a willingness to change—must be taken by us.

Joanne Kanoff, owner of a skin salon, developed the lecture on skin care which I use in my course, and she is also the consultant for this chapter. Skin is the most extensive of your body's organs. It protects the inner organs from foreign elements and helps the body regulate its own temperature.

Your face constantly produces dead cells that must be removed, so you should use either a good scrub or a mask. You must keep your face scrupulously clean. If you apply a used washcloth, a dirty powder puff or even a perspiring hand to your face, you may infect the oil glands that lubricate the skin. Then you will have blemishes.

Your skin also serves to register your emotional state. If you are embarrassed, you blush; if you are angry, you may flush; and if you are frightened, you may turn pale. If you are under stress or excited, you may find your skin telling the world by breaking out in blemishes. Your skin may also register the fact that your diet is poor, your hormones out of balance, or that you smoke or drink.

One of my students had a perfect complexion as a teenager, but after a few years of marriage, her face erupted with angry red splotches. She and her husband had both used their charge cards so frequently that they were receiving embarrassing phone calls and threats from bill collectors. Stress was causing her blemishes. When she and her husband went to a credit counselor and began finding a way to pay off their debts, her face began to clear up magically, too.

A lot of women buy skin products, use them two to three days, then leave them unopened in their medicine cabinets for two weeks at a time. They wonder why their skin does not improve. You must develop a fixed routine, then follow it every morning and night if you want a lovely skin.

Wrinkles, Age Spots and You

Here is a little bit of wisdom to help you remember the importance of skin care:

At the age of twenty, you have the face God gave you.
At forty, you have the face you are working on.
At sixty, you have the face you deserve.

Our skin is much like a flower. We can either care for the complexion God has given us, we can work on it and make it still more beautiful—or we can neglect it and let it shrivel like a rose hip on a thorny stem.

Most of us live in climates where hot, drying sunshine shrivels our skin and splotches it with chloasmata—those yellowish or yellowish-brown patches sometimes called age or liver spots. Cold winter wind also tends to dry out the moisture in our faces. And the ultraviolet rays of the sun may further age our complexions.

There is a theory that the sun's ultraviolet rays are becoming stronger because we have destroyed the layer of ozone that used to screen them from the earth. While this theory has not been proven, it is a fact that dermatologists are finding more dehydration, skin cancers and chloasmata than ever before, and these skin problems are occurring at earlier ages.

As much as we all love the sun and the great outdoors, we should be aware that they can cause many skin problems. If you don't believe this, notice how the areas of your body that are usually covered by clothing remain soft, unwrinkled and ageless. Then compare them to your hands, which are often exposed to the elements. What a difference! In the middle-Eastern countries where women wear veils on their faces, youthful complexions are retained even into advanced age.

By now you may be wondering if it is possible to sunbathe at all. (Who wants to remain cooped up in the house all summer, looking like some spongy-white toadstool, while others go around gorgeously tanned?) The answer is yes, but tan slowly. However, most of us don't have the patience to do that. We want a glorious brownness all at once.

The best way to sunbathe is to expose yourself to the sun only about ten minutes a day. Sun damage to your skin begins at the point when redness begins to appear. Burned skin is like a rubber band that has been left too long in the sun and becomes discolored. If you try to stretch this faded piece of rubber, it will break in two, simply because the elasticity has been destroyed. The natural elasticity of skin is destroyed when it begins to turn red. The face gets lined and leathery. Eventually it has wrinkles.

Age also causes wrinkles. But you don't have to look older than you are! So do protect yourself from the sun. There are many good sun screens on the market. When you choose one, be sure that it has a sun-screen ingredient called PABA. If you apply a sun block (a product that prevents the sun's rays from coming in contact with your skin), you will never burn or tan, for it offers virtually complete protection against the sun.

Many skin problems come from a combination of taking drugs and exposing oneself to the sun. If you sunbathe while you are taking tranquilizers, you may find chloasma spots appearing on your skin. If you are taking tetracycline to cure your acne, your complexion may burn in patches, giving you a peculiar quilted look. Even aspirin combined with the sun's rays may adversely affect your skin. So stay out of the sun as much as possible while you are taking medications.

Prescriptions for high blood pressure, diabetes and epilepsy may cause skin problems even without exposure to the sun. Always ask your doctor what the side effects of drugs can be.

Nicotine makes the small blood vessels contract, preventing the skin from receiving the blood needed to nourish it. Smoking may increase your tendency to wrinkle. Alcoholic beverages can also affect skin tone and muscles.

Skin care routines must become a daily part of our lives, if we are to look our best. In the next chapter we'll look at ways of overcoming special problems.

17

Making the Most of Your Complexion

Adequate moisture is essential for a healthy complexion and must be included in any good skin-care program. For instance, when you put a wrinkled, dried-up prune in a glass of oil, it remains as shriveled as ever. If you drop it into water, it plumps up, to become almost as juicy as the original plum. Your skin reacts the same way. Once it becomes dehydrated, only water can restore the moisture. It is true that creams, oils and waxy products will keep the water that is continually being supplied to the outer layers of the skin from evaporating. But they cannot add moisture. Only water can do that.

Air-conditioning and artificial heat continuously dry out our skin. No matter where we go, we can't escape a drying environment. We can restore humidity to a room simply by keeping a bowl of water in it. Better still, simmer a tea kettle on the stove during the winter. You might want to invest in a humidifier. It will make your face more dewy—and your house plants more luxuriant!

The Trouble With Blemishes

If you are healthy and not under too much stress, if you eat correctly, have your hormones in balance, are not a teenager, and care for your face properly—you probably have no blemishes. But every woman should learn how to care for her skin correctly.

Your complexion has many pores, which are designed to bring oil from the tiny glands at their base to the surface of your skin. Both a whitehead and a blackhead result when a pore becomes plugged. A thin layer of skin covers the top of the whitehead. Whiteheads may be caused by stress or diet.

Blackheads do not have a layer of skin over them. The darkness of the blackhead is caused when the chemicals in the oil of the skin touch the oxygen in the air. This is a chemical reaction. Many people think that a person who has blackheads is dirty. This is not necessarily true. However, the oil in the plugged pore does attract dirt, dust and pollutants from the air. When you press the telephone into your face as you talk, wash with a dirty facecloth or even touch your skin with your hands (even though you just washed them), you are transferring dirt into the open pores.

A blemish (pimple) is a blackhead or a whitehead which has become infected and inflamed, and if you pick or squeeze it, you simply inflame it further. You may spread the infection into your bloodstream, which may then carry the germs elsewhere, causing more blemishes.

If you really can't bear to be seen with a blemish, put warm compresses on it to bring it to a head. *Sterilize* a needle, open the blemish, and allow it to drain by itself. Squeezing can cause scarring.

Another type of blemish, rather uncommon but still possible, is a pocket of oil which collects under the skin. It may result from eating too many dairy or other fatty foods.

Stress-caused blemishes are usually hard, deep, and so painful that they often throb when you bend over. These seldom come to a head. A dermatologist might prescribe tranquilizers for this type of problem. Be sure to ask what the long-range effects will be.

The reason that stress causes blemishes is that your emotions can cause the glands in your skin to secrete oil rapidly and in spurts. The gland becomes plugged with oil below the surface. Many women who never broke out as teenagers start erupting with blemishes at age thirty or so—about the time that they have to care for several small children, a home and a husband.

Good nutrition is a must for a blemish-free skin, just as it is needed for a healthy body. If you have blemishes, you probably should avoid salt, sugar and caffeine. Everyone reacts differently to foods, of course, but many people find that chocolate and cola drinks also cause blemishes.

Be sure to eat plenty of proteins and green, leafy vegetables. Try taking a multiple vitamin. Above all else, avoid greasy foods, such as French fries and hamburgers. Your face could be affected by animal fats even if you don't eat them. If you merely work in a greasy environment, such as a fast-food restaurant, you could develop blemishes.

Skin cells repair themselves while we are asleep, so try to get plenty of rest. If you drink six to eight glasses of water daily and have the proper elimination of food wastes, you should see an improvement in your face within two weeks. To give your skin a clear, healthy look, get plenty of daily exercise so that the blood will flow into your face and cleanse it.

Which Product to Buy

Beyond following good health rules, the most important thing you can do to stay free of blemishes, wrinkles and other skin problems is to follow a regular program of cleansing your face with cosmetics that are right for you. A good skin-care program always includes daily cleansing, freshening and moisturizing.

It is a good idea to use a scrub or mask at least once a week. Some women prefer a mask because they feel that the granules in the scrub tend to enlarge the pores and cause dryness. On the other hand, others find that the scrub actually helps cleanse their pores of soil, while removing dead skin. You must find what works best for you. My skin-care teacher prefers a scrub to a mask, because it requires less time.

There are at least two philosophies about which kind of cosmetics to use. For instance, a product that contains waxes and fillers may be up to 80 percent effective as a sun screen and thus may in time prevent many sun-produced wrinkles. However, these waxes and fillers are considered by others to be harmful to the skin. This opposite view maintains that these ingredients clog and enlarge one's pores, and thus recommends a water-based or water-soluble product. The view that water-based cosmetics actually replace the water that evaporates from the skin—and thus help prevent dryness and wrinkles—is supported by most major cosmetic companies.

Eliminate the use of deodorant soaps on your face. Since they kill the natural bacteria that protect your skin, all kinds of foreign bacteria and fungi are free to invade.

Regular household soaps can be harmful, too. They are very alkaline (and hence very drying). Many contain wax fillers or animal fats, which leave a scum on your skin that cannot be removed, even if you rinse thirty times!

If you must wash your face with soap, use a transparent complexion bar that is made especially for the face. However, most complexion bars contain a large amount of glycerine, which is too drying for most skin types.

What Kind of Skin Do You Have?

Choosing a skin-care program depends on what kind of skin that you have.

Normal skin has a balance of oil and moisture on the surface. Oil comes through the pores and moisture through the sweat glands, to mix on the surface and produce a soft, smooth, dewy complexion. Normal skin seldom has blemishes. To keep it looking youthful, simply stay out of the sun, use good cosmetics and include a moisturizer.

Dry skin is very fine grained. It *feels* dry, taut and tight. Broken veins and dry, flaky patches may be seen. While you cannot see any pores, the skin feels coarse and looks thin.

If you are dry-skinned, avoid anything that will further dehydrate your complexion—such as alkaline soaps. Even water is slightly alkaline. Dry skin requires more emollients, because as the water evaporates from the cells, the cells collapse. The result is wrinkles. Try to keep moisture on your face at all times, and add humidity to your home.

Oily skin shines all the time. There are usually large pores around the nose and chin. Frequently there are blackheads, whiteheads and blemishes. Sometimes there is acne, the most severe form of eruptions. Oily skin may appear sallow or yellowish in color and feel thick to the touch. The oily-skinned person may have few wrinkles, but those she does have will be deep. They result from using very strong and dehydrating cleansers, especially in the eye and neck area.

The goal should actually be to remove only the *excess* oil. By removing all the oil from the skin, the oily-skinned person will only cause her glands to start pumping oil at a faster rate. She may find that a lotion cleanser penetrates deeper than a cream cleanser. Oily skins require moisturizers just as much as do dry skins. There are non-oily moisturizers made especially for them.

Most oily-skinned people should use a scrub or a mask more frequently. These two products refine the pores, stimulate the circulation and help bring impurities to the surface.

Combination skin is the most common complexion type. Usually there is oily skin in the "T" area (forehead, nose, and chin). On the cheeks, eyes and neck lies drier skin. A heavy moisturizer would not be needed in the "T" area, but may be required elsewhere.

Products Available

Once you have chosen good products for your particular skin type, try to get *expert* help on how to use them (not necessarily the saleswoman). Let's look at some of the available products and how they should be used:

Cleanser—removes makeup, dirt and oil and also softens blackheads. Apply this product in an up-and-out movement on the cheeks and chin to avoid pulling your facial skin down and causing wrinkles. When working around the eye, use a circular motion. Start at the tear duct, move over the lid, around the outer corner and in toward the nose. Gentleness is important.

Scrub—designed to stimulate circulation, soften impurities, remove the dead cells.

Mask—designed to stimulate circulation, draw out impurities, tone and firm.

Freshener—removes excess cleanser and oil, may help normalize the pH balance after use of a cleanser. Fresheners help your face accept the moisturizer.

Moisturizer—adds water to skin cells, softens face, plumps cells.

Who should use these products? Virtually every girl from the age of thirteen on up—for it is the years between puberty and the mid-twenties when skin needs the most constant attention to preserve it for the later years.

Always be sure to use puffs made of 100-percent cotton to remove or put on makeup, rather than a dirty powder puff or a paper tissue. The powder puff will carry germs to your pores and create blemishes. The paper tissue contains wood fibers, which scratch the face and break the tiny blood vessels below the surface and may cause permanent damage. Many products which are labeled cotton puffs or cosmetic puffs actually contain part (or even all) synthetic fibers. Be sure that you choose only 100-percent cotton products.

Once you have mastered skin care, you are ready to consider makeup. We'll take a look at makeup in the next chapter. But always remember, skin care must come before makeup!

18

The Magic of Makeup

Properly applied, makeup can be almost as effective as a fairy godmother's wand in transforming "plain Janes" into irresistibly attractive women. In fact, seventeenth-century Englishmen were so aware of this fact that Parliament passed a law to protect men from being unfairly enticed into marrying plain women posing as ravishing beauties.

The law states: "All women, of whatever age, rank, profession or degree whether virgins, maids or widows, shall not . . . impose upon, seduce and betray into matrimony any of His Majesty's subjects by scents, paints, cosmetics, artificial teeth, false hair, Spanish Wool, iron stays, hoops, high-heel shoes, bolstered hips; and shall incur the penalty of the Law in force against witchcraft and like misdemeanors, and that marriage upon conviction shall stand null and void."

If women didn't wear makeup today, it's quite possible that modern politicians might want to pass a law *requiring* its use! After all, life is so much more fun when we can all look more attractive and feel confident. And as the wise old farmer said to his wife in regard to her use of cosmetics, "If the barn needs painting—paint it!"

Don't be afraid to use makeup. You don't have to apologize for enhancing your appearance. In fact, once you learn to use it properly, and others see the subtle but positive effect makeup has on you, they may be encouraged to experiment.

Let me emphasize the "natural look" in makeup, for a well-made-up face is never overdone. Your face should look as fresh and lovely as a dazzling rainbow, but as soft and subtle as a spring bouquet.

Basic Cosmetics and Their Use

Foundation—should match the deepest tone in the skin. (Most women have at least seven, so choose carefully!) A foundation that is too light makes the face look heavier and puffy.

Blush—if applied correctly, may be used to highlight eyes and ovalize the face. But it is very important to choose one that matches your skin tone and shade. If you apply blush too close to the nose, you "lengthen" it. If you place it too low, you make your face appear to sag. If you place it too close to the eye socket, you emphasize wrinkles. Be sure to angle the blush upward on the face. You may also place a light touch of rouge on your temple, forehead and chin to add warmth and sparkle.

Powder—use a translucent product that will not change the shade of your foundation. Avoid chalky looks by using natural or organic powder. Dust powder over your entire face, then dampen a natural sea sponge and lightly pat your entire face to set makeup and avoid a powdered look.

Liner—use only in a thin line or a slightly smudged line, which adds color only to the base of the lashes. A brown shade is softer and more feminine than black. Use a pencil and start with the center of the eye, moving out in a soft, not definite, line. The purpose of the liner is to make your lashes look longer and fuller.

Shadow—a deeper shade on the lid, fading into a softened color reaching up to the brow. Different shades come and go in the fashion world, so be open to experimentation. Get professional advice to help you select the best colors and techniques for you. But again, remember that eye makeup should only bring out the beauty of your eyes—and never be overdone.

Eyebrows—visualize two straight lines running perpendicularly from your tear ducts to the top of your head. If any hairs lie between these two lines, tweeze them out. To determine where the eyebrow should end, place a pencil on your face so that it lines up with the tip of your nose and the corner of your eye and extends beyond it. The eyebrow should arch over the eye and end at the pencil. You may tweeze below the brows for a neat look, but never tweeze above. Remember, if you arch your eyebrows too high, you will look perpetually surprised; if you leave them too low, you will have a scolding demeanor.

Curler—make sure all eyelashes are under the bar and press, holding ten seconds. Then bring the curler farther out on the lash and press again. Try for a sweep, not a tight curl. Apply mascara after curling.

False lashes—if you must add them, they should look natural. Eyelashes must be cut to fit one's eye.

Mascara—use brown rather than black for a softer, more feminine appearance. Apply to the base of your lashes in a rolling motion. Let it dry for a few seconds, then apply a second coat to the tips. Use mascara on the bottom lashes, too.

Lipstick—should complement complexion, harmonize with clothing. A shade that is too light makes the nostrils appear large and the face puffy. Apply by brush for a more finished look that will remain on the lips longer.

Unwanted Hair

You may be surprised to learn that 75 percent of all women have some kind of problem with excessive facial hair. Here are some do's and don'ts about removing it.

Tweezing—should be done only for the eyebrows.

Shaving—dries face, leaves unsightly stubble.

Waxing—tends to be expensive, time-consuming and painful. Also you must suffer an unsightly regrowth period while you are waiting for the hair to grow long enough to rewax. In time, waxing does tend to retard and weaken the regrowth of hair.

Chemical removal—dissolves hair above and below the surface. You must take a twenty-four-hour patch test to be sure that the chemicals will not cause great damage to your skin. Never use these chemicals on irritated or broken skin.

Bleaching—use if you have small amounts of hair. Be sure to make a twenty-four-hour patch test to see if it is safe.

Electrolysis—is expensive but effective in removing hair permanently. Electric current is transmitted into the pore, to make the hair follicle sterile.

Depilation—more expensive than electrolysis, it is the newest type of permanent hair removal. Electric tweezers touch the hair, send a charge through it and sterilize the hair follicle permanently.

What a difference skin care makes in your appearance. Careful use of cosmetics will make you look and feel better. You can learn to work all kinds of magic with makeup and begin to accentuate the positive!

Assignment: Skin Care

1. Analyze the type of skin you have, then shop for the proper kind of product you need. Get professional advice, if possible. Then write out your daily skin-care program and follow it daily.

2. Write down everything you eat for three days. Check to see if you have eaten enough proteins and green, leafy vegetables. If you have blemishes, note whether you have been eating chocolate or drinking colas or consuming other problem items.

Part VII

Hands

Little children were brought for Jesus to lay his hands on them and pray. But the disciples scolded those who brought them. "Don't bother him," they said. But Jesus said, "Let the little children come to me, and don't prevent them. For of such is the Kingdom of Heaven." And he put his hands on their heads and blessed them before he left.

Matthew 19:13–15

19

Lovely Hands Are for Touching!

Maria was born and raised in Lima, Peru, a country where affection is openly expressed with very warm and beautiful body language by almost everyone. When Maria came to the United States as an exchange student, she was to live with an American family whom she was urged to look upon as her own parents and brothers and sisters.

"On the first night, I decided to give all my American brothers and sisters a good-night hug and a kiss," remembers Maria. "I reached out to touch the youngest girl, my new little sister, but as I approached, she drew away. I almost had to struggle with her to catch her. Then I went to the next oldest, a boy. He ran out of the room. I looked at the rest and saw something like fear in their eyes. Then I began to get the message. In the United States, people don't like to be touched or kissed or hugged. I went to bed feeling very sad for them and for myself."

Maria's American family probably *did* want to show her their affection, since for many months they had been looking forward to receiving the bright, attractive young Peruvian in their home—and their hearts were brimming with happiness. But they weren't used to showing their feelings to those outside their own family. *They just couldn't accept a loving touch, no matter how badly they wanted it.*

It is indeed sad that many Americans have not learned to use their sense of touch to express love. We know that a loving hand on a sick person's forehead or a grieving person's shoulder often works wonders. Jesus used his hand to heal the ear of the high priest's servant in the Garden of Gethsemane (Luke 22:51). And the woman who had internal bleeding for twelve years instinctively knew that she would be healed if she could just touch Jesus' robe (Matthew 9:20, 21).

Scientific studies prove that babies who are not touched, caressed, hugged and cuddled often die. Love, expressed through touching, is therefore a basic human need. But why are we so afraid to show our love to others in this way?

Perhaps you don't use your hands to express love because you are afraid of seeming like a clinging vine. However, you will be interested to hear that a study of eighty male and female college students showed that the higher the subject's self-esteem, the more intimate he or she was in communicating through touch, especially when relating to a female. If you pat others on the shoulder or the back, you are proving yourself more relaxed and confident than if you hold back.

A lot of people make fun of those who talk with their hands, saying that they lack word power, but scientists have found that those who have a high rate of hand movements or gestures are actually more fluent than others.

Don't be afraid to use your hands as God intended them to be used! Let them express the love in your heart, the gentleness and gracefulness that reaches out to other people. You will become more beautiful if you do!

If you want more touch in your family, then *you* be the one to instigate it. When sitting beside your husband on the sofa, take his hand. When a child sits beside you, pick him up and place him on your lap, or put your arms around him. Others learn from our loving example. The movements of your hands can attract or repel others. Here are some important do's and don'ts:

1. The proper position of the hand when it is relaxed and at your side is to let the profile show. Your thumb should be relaxed and pointed straight down. The four fingers should be slightly curved toward the body.

2. Never use your fingers to point. If you want to indicate something with your hands, move the whole hand in the desired direction with the palm open and up.

3. Try for more graceful hand movements. When you reach to pick up something, move your wrist first and let the fingers follow. The arm should move in an arch, and the fingers should be relaxed. A bit of practice will make this movement seem more *natural*. Think how ballet dancers move their arms up and down slowly and gracefully, like the wings of a bird. Practice until it does not seem affected.

20

Nail Care

It's as important for your hands to look beautiful as it is for them to move gracefully. You can have more beautiful hands if you determine to work on them. Wear rubber gloves when you use strong detergents and cleaning agents. Give yourself a daily hand massage, using good hand cream or lotion.

If you have splits, breaks, white spots or ripples in your fingernails, check your diet. Deficiencies of vitamins, calcium or protein will show up in nails that look unhealthy. So check with your doctor to see if you need vitamin or other dietary supplements.

Some of the good protein boosters which are available nowadays are low in calories and carbohydrates. They will help improve your nails and general health.

Do you constantly break or tear your nails? Using your fingernails as tools can destroy their beauty. Use the end of a pencil to dial the phone. Grasp small objects like hairpins with the cushions of your fingers. Use kitchen gadgets, not your nails, to pry open the tops of containers. Turn light switches off and on and push elevator buttons with your knuckles rather than your fingers. Use a natural nonalkaline soap for dishwashing.

A well-kept manicure requires only thirty minutes once a week, if it is done correctly. To give yourself a professional manicure in the least amount of time, keep all your manicure equipment together in a shoe box, so that you don't have to spend time looking for it. You will need:

1. A nail file with a very fine, "diamond" filing area. Or if that is unavailable, use an emery board
2. A Q-tip or orange stick for cuticles
3. Cuticle conditioner
4. Nail buffer and conditioning cream
5. Fingernail scissors (not nail clippers)
6. Pumice stone (for calluses)
7. Fingernail polish
8. Hand lotion

Before you start filing, look at your hands to see what nail shapes and colors will be best for you. If you have short, wide fingers, almond-shaped nails will be slenderizing. Avoid an intense shade of polish. Leave an uncolored margin along the sides of the nails, to give the optical illusion of narrowness and length.

If you use an emery board for filing, remember that the dark side (which is rougher) should be used on your toenails. The light side is for your fingernails. When you file, try to achieve a softly ovaled look. A very good length for most nails is one-quarter inch above the back of the finger. Let your nails grow approximately one-eighth inch up on the sides before you begin to file them. Also, file from the side of the nail up to the top of the nail, in one direction only, to avoid tearing.

When coloring your nails, you may want to use a clear base and a top coat, as your polish will then last longer. Brush on polish with three movements to each nail. Start at the center, then do each side. Apply two to three thin coats, letting each dry between coats. Whenever possible, avoid wearing chipped and peeling fingernail polish. Be sure to give your nails plenty of time to dry between coats and after finishing. You may harden the polish by placing your hands under *lightly* flowing cold tap water.

By taking the trouble to keep your hands lovely and feminine and then using them gracefully, you may be able to transmit to others the gentle spirit of God that is within you.

In learning to use the miracle of touch which God has given us, we can pray as did the Psalmist: ". . . the work of our hands, establish thou it" (Psalms 90:17 KJV).

Assignment: Hands

1. Find an appropriate situation this week in which you may touch someone to express sympathy, friendliness or love.

2. Purchase all the supplies necessary for giving yourself a complete manicure as outlined in this chapter. Set aside thirty minutes a week to give your nails regular attention.

Part VIII

Wardrobe Planning

If you can find a truly good wife, she is worth more than precious gems! Her husband can trust her, and she will richly satisfy his needs . . . . her own clothing is beautifully made—a purple gown of pure linen.

Proverbs 31:10, 11, 22

21

How Should You Dress?

If you have never taken the time to analyze your figure and your coloring, you may be choosing clothing that looks wonderful on some movie star or on your best friend—but unattractive on you!

Perhaps you don't feel comfortable wearing something colorful enough to give others enjoyment because you are afraid that such apparel is somehow wrong. You may have been raised to believe that it was Christian to look dowdy.

One of our children knew a boy at school who prided himself on his deep faith. When the other boys wore colorful print shirts with wide collars (the "in" look at that time), he insisted on wearing very conservative, plain shirts with tiny collars and narrow-legged pants (the "out" look). He had the money to buy fashionable clothes, but he preferred dullness. He was also critical of any girl who wore attractive styles. He considered such girls exhibitionists.

What he did not realize was that the other teenagers were so completely turned off by his appearance and his puritanical attitude toward clothing that they could not hear his genuine witness to his faith.

Noted psychologist Dr. Joyce Brothers said in a *Good Housekeeping* article: ". . . a certain kind of 'exhibitionism' is not only normal, but desirable. Liking your own body and wishing to adorn it is a healthy, positive feeling, fundamental to establishing good relationships with the opposite sex. Exhibitionist impulses become a problem only when they're compulsive, when wearing provocative clothes and drawing attention to the body becomes a preoccupation interfering with other more meaningful ways of relating to people" ("Why Some Women Prefer Daring Fashions").

Some well-meaning Christians may think it is best to dress in gray or black or brown, and cut back on the jewelry to keep themselves out of the picture, so that others will be thinking about God and His goodness rather than one's clothes.

If we look dowdy, wear cheap clothing or simply "dress down" so severely that we don't fit into today's world, then others may be thinking about our peculiar appearance, no matter how many religious activities we lead.

One of my students is the wife of a young minister who delights in the fact that she is learning how to be more attractive to others. "My husband loves to see a Christian lady looking nice, pretty and neat while having a good Christian testimony. We can tell such a great difference in the women in our church who have taken The Image of Loveliness course, both in their confidence and personality, as well as in their attractive appearance," she said.

Our associate minister's wife (a color analyst for our course) says, "I have to dress better, look more attractive, no matter where I go, even if it is just to the grocery store. I try to look good because I represent The Image of Loveliness and Joanne. But who is Joanne, compared to the Lord? If we would treat the Lord as a person, we would think, *I need to look my best for Him today."*

Those of us who take our Christian faith seriously will want to dress sharply enough to look like the kind of representatives God wants on this earth!

Some of the women missionaries in our church are given scholarships to attend The Image of Loveliness classes. One missionary, who had been converted after spending several years as a hippie, knew nothing about planning a wardrobe except to dress in shabby jeans and a sweatshirt. Her hair was stringy; she was overweight. Yet, after conversion and schooling, she was representing Christ and the church. She prayed that she would learn the proper way to dress, and enrolled in The Image of Loveliness course. She began to look so wonderful that the light of the Lord seemed to shine from her face!

If you are married, your husband may carry with him throughout the day an image of you as you looked when he kissed you good-bye this morning. Did he last see you as a woman in a torn, frayed robe with a splotch of coffee on it?

If he has to compare that picture of you with the bright, attractive secretaries in his office, or the other trim, well-groomed women on the job, he may not be thinking about how beautiful you are on the inside. After all, he is human. He has five senses, and all of them are working all the time, whether he thinks about it or not! He might be tempted to gravitate to the woman who looks, sounds, smells and feels feminine, soft and beautiful. Married or single—most men like glamour!

The more feminine we women become, the more masculine and gentlemanly a man will be. I remember that the first time I thought of wearing something glamorous for my family, it seemed very unnatural for me. But I decided to sew a beautiful Chinese-red satin long robe and pajama pants and wear them to test their reaction. One day as my husband and family were coming home after school, I put them on and added gold jewelry and slippers. When I heard the car drive up, I held my breath.

My son was the first to walk in. He saw me, stopped in his tracks, and let out a wolf whistle that I didn't think my fourteen-year-old was capable of! The rest of the family was just as enthusiastic! I became a true believer in the importance of glamour in my life.

I agree that looking feminine and glamorous never takes the place of cultivating a loving, gentle personality. But each child *needs* to be proud of his parents. A child feels more secure with a mother who likes herself enough to want to look her best. Today I try to select a glamorous yet very tasteful garment to wear at home for at least one evening a week. I feel I owe it to my family to be as feminine and loving as I can, and this is one way to do it.

There is nothing wrong with wearing black, navy or gray, as these colors do make you look slimmer. But if you wear these dark shades, it is important to add color to your face with makeup. You might possibly add bright accessories for extra glamour.

When speaking of Christian glamour, I refer to something that is much different from the way a nightclub entertainer may dress. Just what does the Bible tell us about a Christian woman's attire? "And the women should be . . . quiet and sensible in manner and clothing. Christian women should be noticed for being kind and good, not for the way they fix their hair or because of their jewels or fancy clothes" (1 Timothy 2:9, 10).

Therefore, the Christian woman should shrink from anything that appears immoral—whether it is too short, too tight, too luxurious, or too conducive to envy, lust and abnormal notice.

This verse may seem a little passé, after emphasizing the importance of glamour and color. But if we have a weight problem and wear clothes that are too tight, we will look larger. If we have large legs (or too-thin legs) and wear our skirts too short, we will then accentuate the less attractive parts of the body. These verses are simply another way of saying, "Look your best."

I am sorry to say that the same nudity that formerly was seen only in some men's magazines is today labeled "fashion" in some prestigious women's magazines. Even though these magazines may portray nakedness as seductive, most authorities agree that a woman is actually more desirable when she is tastefully attired. She leaves to the imagination the question of what she is really like. Being "desirable" should also mean—to both male and female—"desirable to be with."

We can find the right balance between a wardrobe that flaunts our body and one that, by its attractiveness, carries God's perfume to others. "As far as God is concerned, there is a sweet, wholesome fragrance in our lives. It is the fragrance of Christ within us, an aroma to both the saved and the unsaved all around us" (2 Corinthians 2:15).

A friend of mine who vacationed in Hawaii could not resist bringing home some of the beautiful island flowers in her suitcase. When she unpacked, she realized that the lovely fragrance of the flowers had so permeated her clothing that the remembrance of Hawaii would be in her closet for weeks. It is impossible to linger in our Lord's presence without being filled with His perfume. If we spend time with Him, we will be able to carry His fragrant presence wherever we go.

As we choose our wardrobe and work on better grooming, let's remember that we are to look our best, in order that we may be God's beautiful representative. We may not be able to change body build, height, or the color of our eyes. But God has given us perfect freedom to select clothing that can improve our appearance.

One of my students, who had always been rather insecure with others, became aware in my class that she had long been wearing colors that made her look drab. She began replacing her old wardrobe with bright, cheerful, feminine things that were perfect for her figure and complexion. On receiving an invitation from her husband to attend a convention with him, she felt nervous about wearing the new clothes around strangers. But after she returned, she was so excited that she had to write me this letter:

"One man told us his wife thought I was the prettiest woman there . . . . I felt it was quite a compliment for me, a woman over forty who is definitely over the hill!" She soon attended another conference where someone else said, "I just wanted to tell you before I left that you looked like a fairy princess this whole weekend."

When we learn to wear clothes that become us, we can often effectively carry the lovely fragrance of our Christian beliefs to others, bringing inner confidence as we relax and enjoy others.

22

Make Your Wardrobe Work

If we are to look good in our clothes and become more attractive, we need a positive attitude—an attitude which says, "Yes, I want to improve my appearance. I'll wear something glamorous, and accessories I've always avoided. Yes, I will go ahead and do it!" The important thing is to believe that *you can be more attractive!*

A few years ago, when false eyelashes were "in," I decided to treat my own lashless eyes to a pair. Since they looked very natural, most people did not suspect they weren't "home grown." However, now and then someone would look at me critically and ask, "Are you wearing false eyelashes?" I never apologized; I just smiled delightedly and said with a lot of enthusiasm. "Yes, aren't they fun!" It seemed that my answer brought positiveness to the situation.

It is healthy to want to look your best. If we do not want to look better, it may be that an inner solution is needed. Those who work in mental institutions say that it is considered a sign of improvement when a patient who has been suffering from depression requests a mirror and a lipstick.

Roberta followed a straight "A" path to a master's degree. But after many years of studying, she works in a position that does not even require a college degree. She is overweight and wears sloppy clothes. Her hair is stringy and she looks like it's her desire to become "the poster girl for National Acne Week."

It is obvious to others that her appearance is holding her back, but those closest to her don't bother to help her look more attractive because they know that unless she is willing to change, little improvement can be made.

Dressing habits often indicate the mental health of a person. People who wear very bizarre, strange things usually have some kind of problem. When people exchange their sloppy manner of dressing for attractive clothes, this is usually a sign that their self-concept is improving.

Having fun doing things you're not accustomed to, dressing more attractively, using pretty colors and up-to-date styles can help you be happier.

Before looking into wardrobes, let's talk about good grooming— the necessary foundation on which to build a better appearance. Here are some important rules:

1. Bathe and use a deodorant daily. Finish off your appeal to the five senses with a spray of perfume. (Never substitute perfume for deodorant.) If you bathe in the morning and plan to go out again for the evening, use a deodorant once more before evening.

If you cannot bathe for some reason, try a sponge bath, as do missionaries when they have no deodorant available. They add one tablespoon of rubbing alcohol to one cup of warm water and wash all important areas. In this way they remove all bacteria. They feel very clean.

2. Don't neglect to shave your underarms and legs. Do this summer and winter to avoid odor and to be well-groomed.

3. Be sure that all your clothing is clean, including your shoes. Don't forget that the backs of your shoes can look run-down if the heels are worn—even though you cannot see them in the mirror.

4. Be sure that your undergarments are clean and free from safety pins and soil. Mend your slips, bras and panties before you wear them. Maybe your mother always predicted that you would be embarrassed to have pins and dirt show "if you were in an accident and had your underthings exposed." That may be true. However, the knowledge that you are clean and well-groomed down to the skin will help you feel better about yourself.

5. Keep your clothes pressed at all times.

6. Don't let your stockings bag at the ankles or knees.

Most likely you have heard every one of these rules before. But they are so important for us to remember that they bear repeating. Keep yourself clean and neat. Resolve to do it today!

When grooming is mastered, we are ready to *study* fashion. Remember that fashion varies, not just from year to year, but from season to season. One of the best ways of keeping abreast of fashion is by reading a fashion magazine regularly. In this way you will learn which colors are important, the proper hemline length, the "in" shapes of collars, and whether this season's best accessories are flowers in the hair or scarves tied at the hipline.

As a Christian woman, I won't recommend all fashion magazines. While the editors are supposedly fashion leaders, some may also endorse nudity and editorial material of questionable taste. I wouldn't want some magazines lying around on the coffee table for others to see—especially children. But *Vogue Patterns* magazine is excellent. Even if you don't sew, you will enjoy it, as it will enable you to keep up with the latest of fashions, while demonstrating excellent taste.

Also make it a point to attend at least two fashion shows a year—one which models spring-summer clothes, and the other featuring autumn-winter styles. Stores which are fashion-conscious employ a fashion coordinator to produce a top-quality show. You will want to see professional models wear costumes that are accessorized from head to toe. There is no substitute for seeing with your very own eyes the effect of a total outfit as modeled by a professional.

As you are looking at your fashion magazine and attending style shows, keep your own figure in mind. Ask yourself which styles are made for you, and remember that even the top designers occasionally create styles that are not good fashion, sometimes even in poor taste! Unworn clothing hangs in our closets year after year for two reasons: either the color or the style is unflattering.

Sometimes, through years of experience, we feel we know which colors are our best. But it is surprising how many of us are mistaken. In The Image of Loveliness courses, we encourage students to have a color analysis made by the experts who are associated with our organization. The color specialist studies the student's eyes, hair and complexion. She experiments with a wide range of shades and determines the student's color personality. Everyone falls into one of four categories—spring, summer, fall or winter—and receives a chart of the colors which are best for her. Many a "summer" person, who loves orange and yellow, has been surprised to learn that these favorite colors actually muddy her complexion, while soft pink, blue or white bring out a special clarity and softness about her. Once you know which colors are best for you, you will save a lot of money when selecting your wardrobe.

In studying your figure, be aware of these rules to make the most of your physical beauty:

1. Strive to look as tall as possible. If you are short, accept your lack of height, but choose lines that will make you look taller. Most stores select models that are at least 5'8" tall, because clothes look best on tall figures.

2. Strive to look as slim as possible. Of course, a few people are too slim and must add bulk to their clothing to look heavier. But these people are certainly in the minority!

3. Keep your wardrobe in the proper proportion to your figure. In other words, remember your size. If you are short and small, choose small accessories and fabrics with small patterns. If you are tall and have a nice figure, you can get by with larger accessories and big, bold plaids.

4. Remember that the lines of a dress can be used to create illusions. It is entirely possible—and quite desirable—for you to make yourself look your best. A costume can make you look bigger or smaller, depending on whether the dominant lines make the eye travel upward or outward on the figure.

Vertical lines that will make you look slimmer and taller are V-necklines, chains, scarves, long pendants, open shirtwaists, buttons down the center of the dress or a long stripe down the center. The horizontal lines that shorten and make you look heavier include belts, cuffs, two-color combinations, horizontal stripes and fabric with a horizontal weave.

To use the illusion of lines properly again, you must first study your own figure. You know which parts of your body should be smaller or larger, because you measured yourself in the chapter on dieting. (Remember, the bust and hip measurements should be roughly the same, the waist about ten inches smaller.)

Here are a few problems and some tips on how to minimize them:

Extra full at bust, waist or hip—avoid horizontal lines or two-color combinations.

Too short—avoid belts with top stitching that emphasize horizontal lines; fabric that has an almost invisible horizontal weave; double-breasted outfits and patterned skirts. Do wear solid-colored dresses; blouses and skirts of the same color in solids or the same pattern.

Short and slim—wear jackets to the waist or just below. If the jacket line is too long, you will look out of proportion. Good styles are blousons (without bulk), jumpsuits with the belt of the same color, and vests and pants.

Moderately full figure—wear jackets without lapels and avoid detail. Use medium weight, not heavy or thin, fabrics. Choose simple lines with nothing fitted at the waist.

Very large all over—use a simple collar or no collar at all. All lines of the garment should be vertical. The jacket should just skim the body. Do not use big scarves or heavy material. Wear solid colors. Draw attention to the face with color, earrings, and so on.

Tall (correct weight)—wear bigger plaids, shiny fabrics, stripes, layered clothing. Belts of contrasting color are good, unless the person is short-waisted.

Small bust (correct waist, average-to-tall height)—wear double-breasted outfits, horizontal stripes. Large (not too bold) vertical stripes which continue all around the body will make the eye move horizontally and make the bust look larger. Short sleeves, gathers, Empire waist are all good.

Large bust—avoid short sleeves, horizontal stripes, horizontal stitching across bustline. Camouflage with a no-lapel jacket.

Small bust (short height, no waist or hip problems)—use gathers, fullness at bustline. Wear boleros, lots of detail at bustline.

Large bust and waist (average hips, average-to-tall height)—wear straight vertical lines, unfitted jackets, V-necks, blousons. Buttons should all be the same color. Avoid clinging fabrics, empire waistlines.

Large hips (average-to-slim weight, small-to-average bust and waist)—add fullness in the top area. Fullness in the skirt may be used to camouflage the hip area. Even if you are short, and pants are worn, you may use a jacket long enough to cover the hip area.

You can look more beautiful simply by choosing the correct clothing styles for you. Use the illusion of line, the knowledge of fashion and the magic of colors chosen especially for you to become a beautiful woman.

23

Coordinating a Wardrobe

Once you have a grasp of the wonderful things that line can do for you in your clothing, you will no doubt want to rush out and buy a whole new wardrobe. But don't go until you've studied this chapter. Learn to plan your purchases and coordinate your wardrobe. You will not only look better in your clothes, but you will save money, too. Here's what one student wrote to me after learning wardrobe coordination:

"I'd like you to know how great it is to go shopping for clothes now and know what I'm looking for and not be sidetracked by sale signs on merchandise that doesn't fit me. My mother-in-law was so excited about my outline for a new wardrobe that she offered to buy me a good coat for Christmas. I spent days looking and found just what my notebook indicated was right for me—a beautiful camel hair with perfect lines and length. Thank you, Joanne! Your classes will be a pleasure to me for the rest of my life."

Before you go shopping, keep in mind your figure and its problems. In buying ready-made garments, you must select the fabrics, patterns and lines that are just right for you.

When you are choosing any clothing, ask yourself this question: Is this a fad style, for only one season? Is the hemline the proper length to be fashionable next year as well as this? Is the fabric good quality? Is the garment well-finished? Do plaids and stripes match? Are there puckers at the seams? Choose items that can be worn for several seasons.

Selecting clothing is only half the fun of wardrobe planning. You can display your real fashion knowledge by the accessories you choose. Each season I take great pleasure in buying new accessories which will rejuvenate the pantsuits, skirts and dresses I have carried over from past years. To be knowledgeable about accessories, study store mannequins, newspaper articles and some fashion magazines. This year's scarf knotted around the neck may be supplanted by a simple string of pearls next year. You are going to look wonderful all the time with a minimum investment by choosing these fun things that tantalize the beholder like garnishes used by a professional chef.

The Importance of Accessories

There are some general accessory rules which I try to follow. These may be somewhat different from those dictated by fashion magazines, but I feel they are especially suitable for the tasteful Christian woman.

Shoes—should be the same color as the hem of the garment, or darker. With a casual dress or sportswear, you may wear brighter, but not lighter-colored shoes. (You want the entire look to *blend*.) Only wear white shoes with an outfit that is predominantly white. If you wear winter white, you must select a shoe that is suitable for the winter months. You should not wear your white summer sandals in cold months. Actually a leg-colored shoe is more attractive and versatile with summer pastel clothing. Since fashion varies in different areas of the nation, check your local practices for the times when summer white may be used.

Nylon stockings—If you wear dark colors, your stockings should be the same color tone as the shoes or blend with them. Dark stockings are usually worn only in the fall and winter months with dark clothing. Avoid wearing navy or black hose with red shoes. It is always safe to wear leg colors—but *do* be fashionable.

Gloves—used to be on the necessities list, but now are off. For most women, a pair of leather gloves and a pair of warm wool gloves are enough, with perhaps the addition of a long glove for formal evening functions. Avoid pastel and bright colors. Use neutral and deep shades.

Handbags—do not have to match your shoes as long as they blend with your outfit. Invest in a good handbag. If need be, you can dress stylishly with only two good leather bags a year. One might be in tan or deep beige, the other black, navy or brown. Cloth bags are usually worn with sportswear. Straw and linen are generally reserved for spring and summer.

Jewelry—should be button or loop-type earrings in medium sizes for round-the-clock wear. Save anything dangly or sparkly for evening. Earrings and bracelets can effectively add a fresh look to a garment.

Hats—as a whole, are being worn less and less, with the exception of rain hats, beach and straw hats. But, if you love hats, wear them! Choose one according to your proportions. Suede, leather, feathers, fur and velvet are for September through March (in clothing selections as well). Felt may be worn all year round.

Boots—should follow fashion trends. Watch carefully!

Skirt length—should move with fashion. You do not have to go to the extremes shown in fashion magazines, at least until such lengths have become accepted in your area. The goal is to wear a length in which you won't appear to be out of step. And remember, if a longer or shorter length puts your legs at a disadvantage, you don't have to follow the crowd. Wear what is best for you, without going to extremes.

Pants length—should never be high enough to reveal the ankle unless you are wearing a strappy sandal that you *want* to show. Short pants and/or cuffs make your legs look choppy. The best length is to have the hem down on the heel of the shoe, but not dragging on the floor.

Budget Wise

By this time you may be thinking that you must have an unlimited budget for clothes and accessories. Actually, by coordinating and planning your wardrobe, you can make your money go much farther. I used to have closets full of clothes, all different colors of garments with matching shoes and handbags. I thought that having lots of clothes would bring confidence and become my passport to acceptance into society.

The problem with this philosophy was that when Jim received the bills, he would hit the ceiling. As his blood pressure went up, my self-image fell lower than ever.

Today I am striving to be a better steward of the money which the Lord has given us. All my clothes, if placed together, could fit into two to three feet of closet space. Yet I have a "larger" wardrobe than ever. The secret is coordination—and coordination starts with color. Each season I limit to three or four the colors that I will use to build my coordinated wardrobe. In this way, fewer clothes are purchased, but in better quality and nicer fabrics—and with more choice of things to wear!

Unless you can afford to throw away everything in your closet and start fresh (and very few can afford to do that), do not expect to coordinate your wardrobe overnight. It took me three years to assemble a fully coordinated, all-season wardrobe in my closet. Coordinate gradually by choosing a few interchangeable colors and sticking with them. When you replace a garment, be sure it is in one of your chosen shades. Buy or make all separates—pants, suits, skirts and jackets—in the basic colors. (For variety, you may wish to buy an occasional garment in a completely different color.)

Buy nothing but classic, non-gimmicky styles and you can use the same garments several years in a row, perhaps updating them each season with smashing new accessories. Since I sew almost all my own clothes, I can have even greater selection and be more creative. A good bit of advice to all women is to invest in a sewing machine and lessons! Another plus for working with basic colors is that you can dress well with as few as two pairs of shoes (and handbags) if you wish.

Planning a Wardrobe

Here are the essentials for a coordinated wardrobe (with all colors and fabrics working together):

1 three-piece basic solid-color suit (jacket, pants, skirt) in a quality fabric
1 light-colored pants to coordinate
1 light-colored skirt to coordinate
3 colored (plain, floral, or stripe) blouses
2 sweaters (up-to-date cardigan and pullover)
1 basic (solid color) coat
1 shirtwaist basic dress (long or short) in quality, year-round fabric
1 long hostess skirt
1 vest
2 pairs of basic shoes with style and versatility
Lots of scarves
A few pieces of good jewelry

Discipline may have to be learned in buying clothes. Once you see how wonderful you can look, you may really catch the buying fever! But be careful not to overspend.

One day while reading, I noticed that one of the best stores in town was having a tremendous fur sale. Now, it has always been a dream of mine to have a real fur coat. I just *had* to attend that sale, so I asked Jim to come along "just in case" we found a fantastic bargain.

Trying on all those fantastic furs made me feel like the richest lady in town! Every one of them *was* a fantastic bargain, but the price tags were still terribly steep. Yet each touch of those furs was like a caress. I was feeling awfully covetous, so I bowed my head and said, "Lord, should I? You know how much I've loved things like red fingernail polish and furs all my life!"

Getting no real answer, I looked at Jim, who was waiting patiently and not saying a word about expenses and budgets. Typically kind and loving, Jim just said, "It's up to you." That wasn't fair! Wasn't God supposed to work through my husband? And then I almost laughed out loud as the truth hit me. The big stack of dollar bills that would have to be paid for a fur coat could really be used to better advantage for a lot of other things.

Hadn't I been trying to learn discipline and self-control? The fact that Jim granted permission to buy a fur coat gave me an excellent opportunity to learn self-control. Some day the Lord may provide a fur coat. But for now, He has other things to accomplish in my life. Leaving that store without the coat gave me a new peace and a feeling that I was still the richest lady in town! No amount of money can buy that kind of satisfaction.

There is nothing wrong with buying pretty things, but you can have lots of pretty clothes that will make you look pleasingly attractive—while sticking to the budget. I trust that you will learn to spend time on yourself. Study your wardrobe coordination, then go shopping for pretty clothes, wear them and carry the fragrance of our Lord wherever you go.

Assignment: Wardrobe Planning

1. Study your figure. Write down on paper your needs in clothing, taking into consideration your life-style.

2. Check your closet to see if your present wardrobe fulfills those needs. While you are at it, throw or give away all the articles of clothing that you no longer wear.

3. Plan your future wardrobe purchases so that your clothing will coordinate.

4. Purchase or make a tasteful "glamour" outfit, and wear it for your family.

Part IX

Conversation

A soft answer turns away wrath, but harsh words cause quarrels . . . . Gentle words cause life and health; griping brings discouragement.

Proverbs 15:1, 4

24

Training the Tongue

Sally was a very devoted church woman, but she used her tongue to communicate exactly the opposite of what she really wanted to say. When anyone mentioned religion to her, she got into heated arguments, insisting that her opinion was the only possible right one.

"I know I'm correct," she ranted, her face red and her eyes flashing. Then she would quote the Scriptures to prove it. Unfortunately few of those whom she harangued were attracted to her brand of religion. She made Christianity sound as fulfilling as cleaning the oven!

"So also the tongue is a small thing, but what enormous damage it can do. A great forest can be set on fire by one tiny spark. And the tongue is a flame of fire . . ." (James 3:5, 6). The whole third chapter of James has much to say about the dangerous power of an undisciplined tongue, and little wonder!

We usually know that something we've said without thinking sounds wrong the minute the words leave our mouths, but once the words have been spoken, they can't be retrieved. "I'm sorry" are two of the most important words in our vocabulary, when they are sincerely spoken. If we can use our tongues in the true Christian way, we will want our speaking to build others, to bolster them when they are depressed, to compliment them and help them feel good about themselves. We won't want to whiplash them with sarcasm or wound them with gossip.

One of my students complained that every grocery checker at the supermarket always said, "Have a good day," as he handed over her change.

"I know they've all been trained to say that to everybody. It sounds so phony," she complained.

Even if the checkers are saying it mechanically, we should respond positively. If we learn to accept the best in what others say, we'll all be much happier.

"Let your conversation be *gracious* as well as sensible, for then you will have the right answer for everyone" (Colossians 4:6, italics added). Webster's definition of *gracious* is a long one that includes such words as "pleasing, acceptable, marked by kindness and courtesy, tact and delicacy, or characterized by charm, good taste and generosity of spirit." Can you become more gracious in your conversations?

Introductions

Some of the easist formulas to learn (much simpler than what you learned in geometry, but never memorized by so many) cover how to introduce people. Whole books have been written on the subject, but you can do with these basic four:

1. *In general, one person is always introduced* to *another.* If you are introducing two people of the same sex, give the most respect to the older person by saying her name first. Just say, "Mrs. Smith [the older person], I'd like you to meet Mrs. Jones [the younger person]." When said with enthusiasm, "This is . . ." is the warmest way to introduce two people. ("Mrs. Smith, *this is* Mrs. Jones.")

2. *A younger person is always introduced* to *an older person.* If you are introducing two couples, give the names of the older ones first if there is a great age difference. Say, "Mr. and Mrs. Smith [the older couple], this is Mr. and Mrs. Jones [the younger]." Be sure to include first names of your contemporaries.

3. *A man is always introduced* to *a woman.* ("Mary Smith, this is Bob Jones.") If you give the man's name first (an alternate form), say, "Bob Jones, I'd like *to introduce you to* Mary Smith."

4. *A person with a less important title is always introduced* to *a more important person.* ("Mrs. Smith [chairperson of the club], this is a new member, Mrs. Jones.") Check your etiquette books for protocol for dignitary introductions.

Not only our voices but also our body language are important in carrying out an introduction. A man rises when introduced, but a woman may stay seated unless she is presented to someone who is very prominent, someone she has wanted to meet for some time, her host or hostess, or the guest of honor. A very young woman should rise to be introduced to a woman who is a great deal older.

In most introductions, a woman may offer her hand if she desires. This can be a good way to use touch to show respect and warmth to the person whom you are meeting. If a hand is offered to you to shake, do take it!

What is the best response to an introduction? Simply say, "How do you do," and repeat the person's name. A very warm response is an enthusiastic, "I'm very glad to meet you!" Informal groups of adults and teenagers can safely respond with a casual "Hello," or even "Hi." But when there is a big age difference between the two people, the more formal "How do you do" is better.

Sometimes the person who is presented to you says, "I'm so glad to meet you—I've heard so much about you." Accept it as a compliment and say, "Thank you." Even more thoughtful is the person who elaborates (without embarrassing) on the wonderful things he has heard about you.

However, if someone says he has heard a lot about you without describing what he has heard, don't be overly sensitive and assume that it must be bad. To reply, "I hope it was good," or "What did you hear?" can imply a lack of self-confidence and possibly turn a compliment into self-criticism.

After I had lectured to my classes about these *don'ts,* a student and her husband saw me shopping in the grocery store. They decided to have some fun with me. Her husband deliberately looked stern and disapproving when introduced to me.

"I've certainly heard a lot about you!" he said in a critical tone.

I gulped. "I hope it was good," I said, before I could stop myself.

"Well, part of it," he answered. I could feel my shoulders sagging, but then both of them broke out into peals of laughter. That's the way tongues often operate. We don't plan to say the wrong words—they just come out!

Another pitfall to avoid is saying, "Mary Smith, I want you to meet *my friend,* Judy Jones." (This implies that Mary is *not* your friend.) People can be very sensitive. Those who have not learned to love themselves will hear nothing but our unintentional slights, no matter how much we smile and look friendly.

Have fun practicing introductions with your family. You can all learn together. Then when you introduce someone in public, you can do it graciously.

Training our tongues to express our thoughts carefully is only part of the problem in gaining control over this tiny organ. Some of us gossip, talk too much and dominate conversations. Others find that sometimes the tongue just can't quite do the job—and words completely fail us. But there are ways to overcome these problems and make our conversation lovelier.

"Apples of Gold"

A student told me that she was going to have to drop out of The Image of Loveliness course. It was making her ill!

"But why?" I asked her.

"It's all those people. I feel so uncomfortable sitting with them. Sure, they're friendly and nice, but I can never think of anything to say to them. I've tried and tried, but the words just won't come. Now, just thinking about going to class makes me feel so nervous that I am on the verge of nausea."

It was only after spending time alone with this student that I was able to convince her that even if she wasn't a natural conversationalist, she could learn how to talk with others. In fact, I promised her that she would soon learn to look forward to exchanging ideas and information with other people. After much work on her part, she did!

> Like apples of gold in settings of silver
> Is a word spoken in right circumstances.
> Proverbs 25:11 NAS

We can all learn to be good conversationalists. All we have to do is talk to others—the gas station attendant, the cashier at the grocery store, and those with whom we come in contact every day. The more we practice conversing with others, the easier it becomes.

The surest way to get another to converse is to encourage him to talk about himself. Another suggestion is to ask advice of others. For instance, you may say something like, "We are planning a trip to the east. Do you know of any good places to stop on the way?" or "I'm thinking of buying a stereo. Which brand do you think is good?" You will find that asking a question usually starts others talking.

Don't monopolize the conversation with the *smallest* letter in the alphabet—"I." A conversation with "Me, Me, Me" in it tends to become boring and irritating. It's like spoiling a cake by using salt in place of sugar in the recipe—instead of being as pleasing as apples of gold in settings of silver.

Sometimes all we have to do is to listen—really listen—to what others are saying. When a Christian is filled with God's Spirit, he tries to hear what the other person really wants to say, not what his words actually mean. He also listens to the voice of God's Spirit, so that he can be sensitive to that person.

> Like an earring of gold and an ornament of fine gold
> Is a wise reprover to a listening ear.
>
> Proverbs 25:12 NAS

When I used to spend many lonely hours with my two preschool children, my neighbor always managed to arrive at her mailbox at the exact moment I arrived at mine. This woman was usually dressed in a stained housecoat that had safety pins rather than buttons. She would look at me and say in a bitter tone, "All I ever get is bills and circulars. Why doesn't the mailman just skip me?"

I had heard that this neighbor had many problems, and I did not want to have to spend long hours listening to her talk about them. So, I would just smile and say, "Maybe tomorrow will be better," and almost run back up the front walk. Then I would sit inside the house by myself the rest of the day and wonder why I was so lonely!

Realizing that Christians should be interested in helping other people, one morning I decided to let her talk. Enough words poured from her mouth to fill several unabridged dictionaries. And she did have problems! She talked for almost two hours before I could say more than "Really?" or "I'm sorry to hear that."

But something glorious happened after listening to my neighbor. From that day on I had a new friend, simply because I had given her my attention that afternoon. Before long we could dialogue together—all because I had taken the first step by *listening*.

The Do's and Don'ts of Making Conversation

There are several topics which should always be avoided, except with the most intimate friends (and sometimes, even with them!). They are: (1) age (if the person is over thirty); (2) money (its lack or abundance); (3) illnesses or operations; (4) weight; (5) politics; (6) religion.

Maybe you're thinking that I've eliminated every possible thing there is to talk about! Cheer up! Here are some stimulating topics that every woman would be happy to discuss . . . .

Amusing things that have happened to you are always interesting to others. Topics such as fashion, food and decorating appeal to almost everyone. Others will also enjoy hearing about the good and wonderful things that have happened to you or your friends. (No bragging, please!) Everyone likes to be uplifted by happy, positive experiences.

"All living things shall thank you, Lord, and your people will bless you. They will talk together about the glory of your kingdom and mention examples of your power. They will tell about your miracles and about the majesty and glory of your reign" (Psalms 145:10–12).

It has been said that great minds discuss ideas; average minds discuss events; and small minds discuss people. We don't need college degrees to be good conversationalists. "Education" means any area in which we are knowledgeable. Amy Vanderbilt, in her booklet *Now You're Talking,* tells us that by reading the newspaper we can learn about many subjects that will spur a good conversation. If there is no time to read the newspaper from cover to cover, concentrate on these parts:

1. Headlines and the front page (so you will not look blank when others mention a current event in which *they* are interested).
2. Fashion or society page (to keep up with things women discuss).
3. Ann Landers (or similar column, because so many read it). Your opinion makes good conversation.
4. Sports (especially for talking with men).

The husband of one of our students had been invited to be the best man in the wedding of a well-to-do friend. His wife was panic-stricken, because everyone else in the wedding party seemed to move in higher social circles than she did.

"What will I ever talk about?" she wailed to her Image of Loveliness teacher.

"Just remember that every woman, no matter what her station in life, is interested in food or fashion. Talk about some of the things you have learned about nutrition or wardrobe in The Image of Loveliness classes," the instructor suggested.

The student did just that, being careful to do it in a gentle way, rather than acting like an authority and trying to impress others. She was thrilled to find that others listened and seemed to enjoy what she said. She was excited to find herself conversing at ease with people who normally would have made her very nervous. "For the first time in my life, I could relax and enjoy myself in a crowd," she said.

25

Conversational Hazards

As we develop our ability to talk with others, we must be aware that a fast-moving conversation can be much like a golf course—it is filled with hazards. We must constantly be on guard to keep our tongues from leading us into the sand traps of gossiping or taking over and dominating the conversation.

Billy Graham said in his book *Peace with God:* "You are to be radiant. You should be chivalrous, courteous, clean of body, pure of mind, poised and gracious. Silly flirtations, unhealthy gossip, shady conversations should be avoided like rattlesnakes. Your appearance should be neat, clean, attractive, and as much as possible in style, with good taste. Extremes should be avoided in all directions. You should strive to be the ideal gentleman or lady. Your life and appearance should commend the Gospel and make it attractive to others."

Gossip is as prevalent as house dust and much more difficult to remove! Idle talk or mischievous tattle that hurts others also belittles the one who gives it. Psychologists say that gossipers are usually insecure people who dislike themselves. They try to make themselves feel better by making others sound worse.

We should not make fun of others when we are telling a story about something amusing that happened to us. Before saying anything, silently answer these three famous questions: (1) Is it kind? (2) Is it necessary? (3) Is it true? If the story flunks any of these rules, the best thing to do is to talk about something else.

When with someone who is gossiping, change the topic as quickly and tactfully as possible. You might be accused of starting gossip simply because you were listening. "A gossip goes around spreading rumors, while a trustworthy man tries to quiet them" (Proverbs

11:13). But be careful not to act superior, or you'll make others defensive.

In material compiled for the Institute of Basic Youth Conflicts, gossip is defined as sharing *private information* about others with those who are not part of the *problem* or part of the *solution*.

Jesus says, "If a brother sins against you, go to him privately and confront him with his fault. If he listens and confesses it, you have won back a brother" (Matthew 18:15). This does not mean that we should always tell our friends how they should change their lives or their ways, for unsolicited advice is the most deadly kind.

No matter how right or wrong someone is, very few of us have earned the right to tell them about it. Even when we *have* earned the right to say what we feel to a friend, we still have to say it very cautiously. Possibly we could start by asking if he is a good friend of ours. If he answers yes, then in time (if our talk is absolutely necessary), in great love, we may tell him our feelings and our hurts. "Help me, Lord, to keep my mouth shut and my lips sealed" (Psalms 141:3).

Another problem in conversing in a group occurs when one person does all the talking. "Don't talk so much . . . . Be sensible and turn off the flow!" (Proverbs 10:19).

Make every effort to draw out a person who isn't getting "a word in edgewise." Try asking her opinion about a subject, or give her a compliment, but don't press too hard. Attempt only three times to draw a response, for we do not want to appear pushy in our attempt to draw out others.

It is impolite to whisper or giggle when someone else is speaking. The speaker may think he has said something wrong to cause our amusement, and he might become distracted. If you do begin to giggle at an inappropriate time, excuse yourself and leave the room until you regain your composure. Then when you return, it may be best not to sit next to the one who made you laugh. You may also need to apologize to the speaker or the one in charge.

Some helpful rules regarding conversation are:

1. Don't interrupt or cut in on others' conversations.

2. Watch the faces of those with whom you are speaking, to see if you are annoying them.

3. Establish eye contact; but don't stare.

4. Our language should reflect gentleness. Use "I prefer," "This is my opinion," or "This works for me," rather than insisting that

only one's own ideas are correct. Being dogmatic or opinionated will cause others to become defensive. "Happy are those who strive for peace—they shall be called sons of God" (Matthew 5:9).

5. Give credit where credit is due. "Betty has a great idea for a fund-raising drive." Or "Oh, I'm so excited about the way Sue showed me how to decorate this wall."

6. Listening to another's complaints and suggestions regarding our manner of speaking may also help us become better conversationalists.

7. Be supportive. Use "igniter" phrases such as: "Great idea!" "Good for you!" "You can do it!" "I'm so pleased with what you've done!" "You're beautiful!"

It takes thought, determination and practice to make our conversational graces perfect. But the more we speak, the easier conversation becomes.

"Even before a word is on my tongue, lo, O Lord, thou knowest it altogether" (Psalms 139:4 RSV). Ask God to tell you if what you want to say reflects *His* beauty and goodness!

26

Listen to Your Own Voice!

A woman may be a great conversationalist, may have beautiful hair, attractive skin and perfect fingernails—but if her voice sounds harsh, the whole picture of loveliness can be ruined.

It is true, however, that many of us don't realize how we sound to others! This is because we can't hear our own voices with accuracy. If you want to hear how you sound to others without a tape recorder (which, after all, does have its mechanical distortions), cup your hands around both ears, pushing them slightly forward. If the sound of your voice is not as pleasing as you'd like it to be, you can train yourself to pitch your voice lower, to speak slowly and calmly or to be more enthusiastic.

Several years ago I would not have dreamed of appearing before an audience. But then I learned to modulate my voice so that it would be more pleasant. Now I speak before hundreds of audiences each year and enjoy it! So can you!

Authorities in the subject of speech tell us that most people do not move their lips, tongue and jaws enough to communicate correctly. We need to have proper enunciation and enthusiasm, however, if we are to be effective conversationalists. But that takes practice.

A good exercise would be to open a book and read it in a whisper for five minutes every day. Project your whispered voice with only your lips, tongue and jaw! This increases skill in correct enunciation.

Dorothy Sarnoff, noted voice teacher and speech consultant, suggests talking into the crease of a magazine to test your voice for tonal quality. Does it sound harsh? Does it have a warmth of tone? As you speak, do you have interesting pacing?

Our ears are sensitive to high sounds, and a lower voice usually creates a more positive response and is pleasing to the listener. Therefore, we should always try to pitch our voices low—especially when we get excited—since women have a tendency to raise their voices when emotionally stimulated.

In several biblical passages (such as Ezekiel 43:2), the voice of God is described as sounding like abundant waters or a magnificent waterfall—soft and soothing, yet inspiring and dynamic in its quality. I am sure that He would want our voices to soothe and inspire others as well.

When you stand in front of an audience, do you find your knees trembling and your voice wavering? You can overcome stage fright! Take your mind off yourself by counting the number of hats, corsages, or blondes you see in the audience. Or pick out a face (but don't stare) and speak to it as if you were talking one-to-one.

Remember to smile and sound happy and pleasant. Try to aim for enthusiasm, except, of course, in moments of sadness or when discussing very serious subjects.

Know your subject, so that you can speak with authority. Be prepared for questions. To avoid stage fright you might want to spend time before the speech, picturing yourself speaking calmly and unafraid. Start speaking to small groups and gradually work up to larger ones. Practice speaking at home, so that you will have confidence when you are around others.

When Moses was chosen by God to deliver the Hebrews, he told the Lord that he was not eloquent enough to do the job. Even when God promised that He would put the words in his mouth, Moses insisted that he could not speak well. Finally he angered God by his disbelief. And so, God made Moses' brother, Aaron, the spokesman (*see* Exodus 4:10–16).

By simply believing God's promise to Moses, we can become better conversationalists. We can demonstrate His love and kindness through our words and actions more effectively if we not only believe that He has given us the power to speak well, but also practice using the rules presented in this chapter.

If you allow the warmth in your touch and the sparkle in your eye to communicate the beautiful life bubbling within you, and ask God to love His listeners through you, watch out! For God's love is the most beautiful and dynamic force in the universe.

Assignment: Conversation

1. While you are in a restaurant, grocery store, or other public place this week, *listen* carefully to what people are discussing. Think of questions you could ask these people to lead them into discussing *ideas* rather than *persons*. Write your answers down in your notebook, then use them in your next conversation.

2. Speak to two people that you have never spoken to before. Through your comments, show them that you love them.

3. The next time you are with someone who starts to gossip, change the subject immediately!

Part X

Etiquette

Be careful how you behave among your unsaved neighbors; for then, even if they are suspicious of you and talk against you, they will end up praising God for your good works when Christ returns.

1 Peter 2:12

27

Chivalry's Not Dead Yet!

Recently, an influential Christian businessman flew to our city to discuss business with me during lunch. I found living proof that chivalry is not dead—it is alive and well! After lunch, this respectable gentleman insisted on accompanying me to my car. He not only took my car keys and opened the car door for me; he also put his hand under my elbow to steady me as I entered. He then handed me the car keys and closed the door.

His good manners reminded me that my thoughtful husband is not the only outstanding Christian gentleman who treats every woman with the thoughtfulness God intended.

Perhaps you are thinking, "No man ever did anything like that for me. If chivalry isn't dead, it must have slipped into a coma!" Could it be your own fault, and not that of the men in your life? The last time you had a date or went out with your husband, did you sit in the car and wait for your escort to open the door, or did you immediately jump out? The last time you dined out, did you give your own order to the waiter, or did you tell your male companion what you wanted and let him relay the information?

Etiquette rules are changing with our relaxed society, but if a man offers you his seat on the bus, do accept it with graciousness. (In light of the current discussions about equal pay and job opportunities and other equal rights for women, many people feel that a man should not be expected to extend special courtesies to women.) Most men want to show their thoughtfulness by protecting us, but so often we don't give them the chance. Their kindnesses are often squelched by our independent attitudes.

Recently our daughter met a young man from Gambia, a small country in western Africa. He is attending college with her in the United States. They have become good friends.

At Christmas, she found a small box and a card in her mailbox.

On opening them, she discovered a beautiful Christmas card and an exquisite necklace from this young man. At first she was a bit taken aback. She hoped she had not led him to think she was more than a good friend. Slightly embarrassed, she was at a loss as to what to do about it.

The next day the problem solved itself. Before she could say anything, he stopped her. "Don't say a word, please. Just don't say anything," he said. "Let me speak first. It was *my* pleasure."

The directness of his statement silenced her for a moment, and she then stammered that at least she wanted to say thank you. He just shook his head and surprised her even more.

"In my country, everyone, small children to old people, give gifts at Christmas," he said. "I have no one to give gifts to. I know very few people here, and my family is in Africa. You are my friend, and again I say that it was *my* pleasure."

Then he added, "Why is it that American women cannot accept gifts or common courtesy? When you offer them a chair, they refuse it. When you try to be courteous, they feel uncomfortable or ignore it altogether. Please realize that I like being courteous to women, and I give gifts because I *want* to."

This example can be a valuable lesson for all of us. If a man wants to open a door or offer you a seat, respect him enough to reply with a simple "Thank you." It may not be only out of deference to you that he does it, but also because it is *his pleasure!*

A friend had proof that many American men feel the same way as the young man from Gambia. One Sunday she was invited to tell the congregation at her church about The Image of Loveliness classes. For fear of offending some people, she almost didn't say that the course encourages "more feminine" behavior, so she merely stated: "I believe women have a role to play, and so do men. The more ladylike and feminine a woman is, the more masculine a man becomes."

She wrote to tell me: "Joanne, I couldn't believe the response! Men were shouting 'Amen,' and 'All right!' In fact, more men came up to me afterwards and thanked me for saying that—young men, middle-aged men and grandpas! Several men asked if there was a course for them, and even asked if they could be the instructor!"

It is not unusual to receive phone calls from teenaged young men, as well as husbands, encouraging us to continue to share the importance of being a gentleman. To help encourage a man to express courtesy toward you, here are two simple rules to follow:

1. Always show your pleasure and gratitude when a courteous act is performed for you. Saying, "Thank you," for even the smallest gestures will make him feel appreciated and encouraged.

2. Slow down a bit and give him the chance to help you, instead of always being two jumps ahead—so he won't have to pole-vault over the hood of the car to open the door for you!

Don't act "slightly helpless" on the job, as it is your duty (and to your advantage) to be every bit as efficient as the men at work. But you can still be both businesslike and gracious with your male co-workers.

If you have been guilty of unfeminine behavior with your husband or boyfriend, you may want to ask his forgiveness and express your desire to change by saying something like, "I have come to realize that my behavior toward you has not been very feminine and that my impulsive and independent attitude may have hurt you at times. So I've come to ask, 'Will you please forgive me?' "

Then go on to explain more specifically how you wish to change: "I should be sitting in the car and letting you open the door, allowing you to order for me in restaurants, and allowing you to help me on with my coat. I'm sorry I didn't know that before. I'll do my best to remember it from now on."

This approach *does* work, but your mate may not become a Sir Walter Raleigh overnight, as it takes practice. Allowing "your man" to become a gentleman is a great way to bring romance back into a relationship. Try it—you'll like it!

One businesswoman I know was sure that her husband didn't want to treat her as a lady. Their marriage had all the romance of a daily dishwashing routine. But when her husband noticed that she was becoming more feminine and proving it by her actions, he was so delighted that he expressed his affection by bringing her flowers.

Of course there are times when the rules of chivalry must be bent to conform to the modern world. If my husband has to double-park downtown in order to drop me off, he can't be expected to get out into the traffic to open the car door for me—or he might be without a limb! If you are a secretary, you won't expect the boss to get up from his desk when he calls you into his office. *Common sense* and sound judgment are most important while making a great effort to let our men be the gentlemen they desire to be.

To Be a Lady, Act a Lady

Many passages of Scripture tell us that the man should be the head of the household, over the woman. Being a lady is one very pleasant way we can obey. Both you and your husband will love it.

Being a lady should not mean that you must avoid wearing Levi's, riding a motorcycle behind your husband or boyfriend, or climbing trees—if that's what you like to do. Being a lady simply means that you should have an outer glow, a *feminine approach to life*. Grooming yourself well, having consideration for others, watching the way you walk, sit, and stand and being in good taste no matter where you are—all these will make others enjoy your company every moment of your life.

A few guidelines to follow when becoming a truly beautiful woman are:

1. *Avoid vulgarity.* "Dirty stories, foul talk and coarse jokes—these are not for you. Instead, remind each other of God's goodness and be thankful" (Ephesians 5:4). You may at some time find yourself attending a business or social gathering with your husband when the air starts to turn blue with off-color jokes. You may not be able to leave without hurting your husband. But if you stay, remain poised and gracious without appearing to be too interested in the so-called humor.

2. *Avoid using your femininity to inconvenience others.* A lady is always on time for appointments and meals. If you see that you will be unable to keep an appointment with your beautician or dentist, be courteous enough to call and cancel. If you do not, you are costing them money in unused time. If you are invited to dinner at someone's house and find that you must arrive a few minutes late, telephone the hostess to tell her. (In some foreign countries and some areas of the United States, it is "impolite" to arrive on time. Be sure to check out the local customs.)

Never arrive before the invited time. Even being fifteen minutes early is enough to frazzle a hostess who is counting on using every last second to make the meal and evening an enjoyable time for her guests. If you arrive too early, it is more considerate to wait in the car. Drive around the corner and park, so she won't have to wonder why you are sitting outside.

3. *Always write a thank-you note to the hostess.* I cannot overemphasize the importance of showing your appreciation to the hostess for a party or time spent with her. If you would be a loving, gracious person, you *must* write thank-you notes, even for a simple dinner.

Sign your notes with "Love," "In appreciation," and so on. Never end with an abrupt signature.

This letter from a grateful husband brought tears to my eyes:

"Dear Joanne . . . Just a short note to tell you that I appreciate all you have done for my wife and, subsequently, me. I married a precious rose, but you really made her blossom. Since she took your course and then became an instructor, I have had the pleasure of watching her change drastically. She is all she teaches, every moment. When she goes anywhere, all eyes turn toward her; when she speaks, people listen; and when she is present, everyone is infected with her enthusiasm. Thanks again!"

You, too, can give others priceless gifts by writing thank-you notes and letting others know you appreciate what they've done for you. You can also reward your husband with ladylike behavior, which will make him feel like a king. Work to achieve the softness, femininity and purity of a beautiful person!

28

Manners Versus Etiquette

What is the difference between good manners and proper etiquette?

Manners are defined perfectly by the Golden Rule: "Do unto others as you would have others do unto you." As far as I am concerned, manners are nothing more than making the other person feel at ease. When you say good morning to the mailman, are pleasant to the person taking the telephone survey and courteous to the department store saleslady, you are using good manners.

Many people think that you only have to consider manners on formal occasions. They dust off Emily Post when company arrives and hide her away on the bookshelf when only the family is around. If you are kindhearted and thoughtful, you will rarely be guilty of bad manners, even if you don't know all the rules of etiquette.

Etiquette simply includes the rules that experts have made to deal with specific social situations. A knowledge of these rules will help you relax, feel more confident and enjoy yourself at a formal banquet or at a party. And so, we will look at some of these rules in this chapter.

Good manners may require breaking one of the formal rules of etiquette, because consideration for others *must always come first.* Queen Victoria once entertained a foreign official at an important state dinner that consisted of several courses. Before the dessert was served, fingerbowls were placed before everyone. The honored guest, when presented with this strange new "dish," promptly drained the warm water in one gulp. The gracious queen, rather than have her guest suffer embarrassment, immediately picked up her own fingerbowl and delicately sipped its contents! She broke the rules of etiquette in order to practice good manners and show consideration for her guest.

If a group of bedraggled and dirty people came to my house for dinner, I would probably don Levi's rather than a hostess gown (though I would be clean, not dirty!). If they sat on the floor, I would sit there also. I would not be practicing good manners if I overdressed and then insisted on sitting above them on the sofa.

Entertain and Enjoy It!

Often we clean up our houses and then never share them with others. Clearly God wants us to *enjoy* other people, for the Bible says, ". . . And get into the habit of inviting guests home for dinner or, if they need lodging, for the night" (Romans 12:13).

Do invite others into your home! Or, if you can't do that for some reason, invite someone for lunch or refreshments at a restaurant. Don't be afraid to entertain. Many people do not entertain at home because they are afraid their houses will never be clean enough. We need to put away our pride. Guests will not expect a spotless home. They just want to enjoy our company.

We should seek not to impress others but to serve. Invite those who are lonely, who need to relax or laugh. When you are planning to entertain, ask yourself, "Whom do I need to *serve?*" From the moment our guests walk into our house, our purpose should be *to put them at ease.* People need to be shown that we are glad to be with them.

When you see someone, always say a word of welcome. No business is ever more important than a smile that says, "Oh, it's so good that you are here!'' Many people will feel rejected if a greeting is not given. A great healing can be accomplished if you say, ''It's wonderful to see you.''

If the idea of entertaining with a formal dinner party overwhelms you, try inviting friends for good talk with simple refreshments on Sunday evening. Or practice a formal dinner party on your family before you try it with guests. Personally, I think everyone should have one dress-up dinner at the dining table for the family at least once a week. Children will learn to be comfortable in a formal setting.

Set the table with your best china. Make a flower arrangement. Wear a hostess gown and let the children dress up, too. Turn down the lights and burn a candle, even if your husband claims you are just trying to hide food that is scorched—or that he can't see what he is eating! Chances are he won't admit that he enjoys the occasion, but inwardly he will be touched that you have made such a nice evening for him.

One student wrote this letter: ''Last Wednesday after etiquette class, I stopped and bought a bouquet of red and white carnations and a white lace tablecloth. I made a red tablecloth and napkins to match and set my table with tablecloths, red candles, napkin rings, a bread knife, and so on. It just looked so lovely!

''I tried your hint about getting my husband out of Levi's, and he wore his dress slacks all day long, and the girls were told they had to wear dresses. There weren't even any complaints! I was amazed. We spent the day with just our four kids, and my husband was especially appreciative of the atmosphere. So not only did it look lovely; we felt lovely and beautiful.''

At the Table

Our conversation is the most important element in any situation. But knowing proper table manners can help us feel more confident. Instead of worrying about which fork to use, we can be free to enjoy ourselves and others.

Here is a brief list of some basic table manners. As you read and study them, always keep in mind that they were designed for practical and aesthetic reasons, and are not an end in themselves.

Cutting food—cut in one direction only. Don't see-saw, as you might make a rickety table shake enough to cause dishes to overturn. Only cut one or two bites of meat at a time.

Using a fork—Don't spear any food (unless dining "European-style"), except bites of lettuce and other foods which are impossible to pick up by placing the fork underneath and raising them to your mouth. You may use pieces of bread as a pusher, but don't sop with them!

Plate passing—pass plates or bowls counterclockwise (to your right) on the first time around.

Salt and pepper—always pass together, even though someone asks only for the salt.

Butter dish—always place a butter knife with it. The knife stays with the butter plate as it is passed. Use the knife to cut off a piece of butter for your breads and place it on your bread-and-butter plate. If you do not have a bread plate place the butter on the salad plate. If that, too, is missing, place it on the dinner plate. Then return the butter knife to the butter dish.

Eating fried chicken—If served picnic style (either outside, or inside, on a TV tray or in an informal manner), chicken may be eaten with the fingers. Otherwise, use a knife and fork to remove the meat from the bones.

Lipstick—may be applied in public, provided you *do not* use a mirror or compact. Simply lower your head, and with three to four quick swoops (which you may want to practice at home), apply lipstick. You will look better for the remainder of the social event, and your actions will be accepted.

Elbows on table—This rule has been relaxed. You may gracefully put your elbow on the table if you are carrying on a conversation after the dinner and you must lean forward to be heard. Sometimes you look too stiff if you hold your arms under the table!

Trimmings—Gravy should be put on the meat, potatoes or rice, while the condiment, pickles and jelly go at the side of whatever they accompany. Olives, radishes or celery are put on the salad plate. Rolls go on the salad dish if no bread plate is available.

In order to learn about formal table settings, it would be a good idea to check out from your library a good etiquette book. (You will be interested in other rules of etiquette too. In The Image of Loveliness classes, we practice many of them—such as how to eat at the table; put on and remove coats and gloves; carry handbags properly, and enter and exit gracefully from a car.)

I want to encourage you to take the time to study etiquette. But do remember that it is *more important* to practice good manners and be considerate of the feelings of others. You will feel relaxed and happy around almost everyone when you do.

Assignment: Etiquette

1. Have a talk with your husband, explaining that you want to become more of a lady. Tell him you're willing to let him open doors and help you with your coat, and so forth. The next time you go out together, slow down and show your appreciation.

2. Explain to your family that you are planning a formal dinner party just for them. Tell them some of the rules you have learned. On the evening of the big day, set your prettiest table. Work for an intimate holiday mood, and don't forget to wear a glamour outfit yourself!

3. If you don't own a book of etiquette, check out one from the library. Review all the rules about table settings, food passing and dining etiquette. But work on loving conversation, which is more important than following all the rules.

Part XI

Woman–God's Idea!

I am the door; if any one enters by me, he will be saved, and will go in and out and find pasture. The thief comes only to steal and kill and destroy; I came that they may have life, and have it abundantly.

John 10:9, 10 RSV

29

Right Side Out

I will never forget the day I walked down the runway at the Mrs. America pageant. The sparkling crown of Mrs. Oregon on my head proclaimed me lovely to look at and beautiful in my relationship with my family and others. The smiles, congratulations and warm embraces from all those around me seemed to lift me up in love.

I couldn't help crying a little as I thought about how God had changed me, the woman who used to have no friends, who had a messy house and a self-image with a minus rating. Remembering those dreary days made it easier for me to answer the question that the judges of the Mrs. America contest sent me in the mail a few days before leaving for the competition.

"What is the most important and thrilling thing that ever happened to you?" they asked in order to prepare me for the interviews at the competition.

My first thought was to say, "The day I married Jim." But then I thought about the birth of our two children, Deanna and Bob. Didn't our children mean more to me than anything in this world? I started to write about them.

Then I stopped. Becoming a Christian and learning to be beautiful on the inside—that was the most wonderful thing that ever happened to me! Without that miracle in my life, I would never have entered the Mrs. America contest in the first place. I would still have been miserable, friendless and unattractive. And so I answered, "As a Christian woman, the most important thing that ever happened to me was when I asked God into my life through faith in Jesus Christ."

As I appeared for my Mrs. America interview and sat before the judges, my stomach was churning with nervousness. The judges knew that I taught a good-grooming course. Wouldn't they expect me to have a flawless appearance and complete poise? Furthermore, one of the judges was a psychologist. If I didn't feel good about myself, he could tell it by the way I sat in my chair or walked into the room. I was feeling very excited and hopeful—but nervous—as the questioning began.

"What's the most important element of beauty?" one of the judges asked. I sighed with relief, because that question was not difficult to answer.

"It's the beauty within," I said. "This comes from a personal relationship with God through faith in Christ."

Wrong Side Out

So many women today think they have to depend on makeup to look their best—believing that enough use of cosmetics can make one beautiful. But without a knowledge of God's love and acceptance, they are just about as attractive as a luxurious brocade—viewed from the wrong side.

The first thing I did when going away to college was to buy lipstick and makeup, forging the true pathway to beauty. Before long the dresser drawer was full of cosmetics. I worked on two majors in college. One was in education, the other was in perfecting my appearance so that I would always be beautiful and happy.

And for a while, I *was* happy, deliriously happy. I was caught up in a whirl of dates, sports events and all-girl get-togethers in the dorm, where we shared beauty hints—such as how best to roll our hair and apply makeup. Life was just plain fun. Besides, I was in love with the neatest man in the world, the dark-haired football player who was later to become my husband.

It all started that gorgeous spring day while I was a senior in high school. I visited the campus with my twin sister, Judy. We were walking around the student union building, when Jim laid aside his Ping-Pong paddle right in the middle of the game.

"Wow," he said to his friend (who soon after became my brother-in-law), "who are they?" Suddenly we found ourselves with two handsome tour guides! Every time Jim looked at me, I almost melted, but I tried not to be affected in an obvious way. Was it possible that he really liked me? Jim picked a solitary plum blossom and handed it to me, then asked me for a date that evening. From then on, we dated steadily.

Jim was not only good-looking, but I admired his dynamic inner strength that came from his deep personal relationship with Christ. Before I knew it, I was head over heels in love, and he loved me, too. We met in May and were engaged the following November. (The plum blossom he gave me the first day we met is still in my memory book, more than twenty years later. I suppose I am just an incurable romantic!)

We were both so much in love that I assumed we would be married and live happily ever after. We did get married, but the "ever after" only lasted awhile. Within three years we had two children, and Jim began teaching in a Christian high school in Salem, Oregon, while I stayed home with the babies.

But something was terribly wrong. My happiness had somehow turned into misery and boredom. Most of my time was spent changing diapers, picking up toys, and doing monotonous housework. Even though I loved my family, something was missing in my life. I tried to fill the emptiness with selfish desires—gossiping, envying, lust, jealousy and lying.

I tried to dress up for Jim when he came home at the end of the day, but it seemed to me that Jim never told me I was beautiful, as he did before we were married. And I was always so tired! I slept ten to twelve hours a night and still didn't seem to have the energy to do anything about the dust that curled up under the furniture—except to wish it would go away. To forget about my misery, I began to nibble between meals. My mirror told me that I was quickly gaining weight.

What on earth had happened to the college girl who had felt so attractive, or the twelve-year-old Joanne who had vowed to be beautiful inside and out? I certainly didn't *feel* lovely anymore.

As my depression deepened, I would look in the mirror and think, "God, You really goofed when You made me." I wanted to blame someone, even God, for my miserable conditions. The more time I spent hating myself and blaming others for my dowdiness, the less time I had to think about the fact that I did not have many friends, proven by the fact that the telephone seldom rang for me anymore.

Of course I had acquaintances. I saw other young married women talking and laughing together at church and wanted to be liked by them. But none of them seemed to want to say more than "Hello" to me.

"Christians are supposed to love each other," I complained to Jim after returning from church one Sunday. "Those women at church aren't even friendly. What hypocrites!'' And before long, it seemed that I was always too sick to go to church on Sundays. I was never ill any other day of the week, but on Sundays I felt so terrible that my husband had to take the children to Sunday school himself.

I sat at home, desperate for companionship but unwilling to take the first steps toward making friends. Every time I mentioned another woman, it was only to point out all her flaws. Unconsciously I was trying to make others look bad so that I could feel good about myself. No wonder I became more and more depressed!

Years later, I heard evangelist Bob Hobson say something about his past that described exactly the way I felt during those years.

"Dying was not my problem," he said. "Living was." I was not living, because I had not yet yielded my life completely to God. I had been raised in a Christian home, but had not accepted myself, nor let God take over my life. Inside, I was not beautiful at all. Sometimes it seemed I was just passing time until I would be through with this dreary life.

God's Way Out

God's love is so steadfast and His patience so great—He used even my misery to cause me to take a very important step. Wishing that I could look beautiful and have friends again, I enrolled in a self-improvement course. Listening to the teacher tell about grooming and posture helped me gain enough self-confidence to take a good look at myself.

"Wow! That fat lady in my mirror must be me!" I gasped, as I determined to go on a diet and *stick with it!* I eventually started to lose weight and began liking the image I saw reflected in my mirror. As I started studying makeup and practiced better posture, I began feeling so much better about myself that I decided to be a fashion model. Mastering the art of pivoting and walking gracefully down a runway, throwing a shawl around my shoulders and posing for photographers with perfect poise paved my way into the professional modeling fields.

Now I told myself I was right side out. Wasn't I pretty on the outside? Wasn't my paycheck proof that I was beautiful? But inside, there was still a great, overpowering ache. Something was *still* missing.

Searching to find what it was that I needed, I began to read inspirational books and study my Bible, and I began to realize that the inside of my head and heart were ugly! How could I be attractive to others when I was so aware of the ugliness in my soul? How could I be motivated to love others, as Jesus asked me to do, when I concentrated on their faults?

Where was the sparkle in my eyes, the lilt to my walk, the genuine reaching out to others that would make me truly lovely? It was not to be found in makeup, posture and clothing. I had concentrated on exterior beauty so much, and reserved no time for developing the inner me.

"Do not be conformed to this world but be transformed by the *renewal* of your mind, that you may prove what is the will of God, what is good and acceptable and perfect" (Romans 12:2 RSV).

While reading Genesis, a verse that I had heard and read many times seemed to leap off the page to me: "Then God said, 'Let us make man *in our image, after our likeness;* and let them have dominion over the fish of the sea, and over the birds of the air, and over the cattle, and over all the earth, and over every creeping thing that creeps upon the earth.' So God created man *in his own image, in the image of God, he created him;* male and female he created them" (Genesis 1:26, 27 RSV, italics added).

Me? Made in the image of God? I could hardly imagine such a thought. Didn't I have a tendency to gain weight and a bad habit of belittling everyone around me? Yet the Bible said that God had actually implanted within me *His own potential for a unique loveliness that could reflect His very own image.* All I had to do was commit every being of my life to Christ, allowing Him to become all He wants to be in and through me.

In prayer, I thanked Him that He accepts me, unconditionally, with all my faults. I don't have to change in order to receive His acceptance—I don't have to prove myself. God loves me unconditionally. I gave Him my will and invited Him into my heart as *Lord* of my life. A great relief warmly filled my life, and I knew that things would be very different. At last I knew that I was right side out.

30

A Way for You

As I stood by the hospital bed staring down at my husband, the tears rolled down my cheeks. How could this terrible accident have happened?

When Jim left the house that morning, he had been in an unusually happy mood. After months of training, he had been certified to become a commercial pilot, and he had already made application for a flying job. Meanwhile, he was helping a friend in construction work. Little did I think that the next time I would see Jim, he would be in the hospital with an I.V. draining silently into his arm.

"When the backhoe hit him, he was thrown against a cement wall, receiving blows to both sides of his head. He has lost half of one ear," the doctor told me. "It's a miracle that he is alive."

All I could think of was to thank God that Jim was living. But later the doctor said that it would take almost two years of plastic surgery before his ear would be back to normal. Then we learned that it was doubtful if Jim's ear could ever hold a pilot's earphones for long periods of time.

"Why, Lord, why?" I kept praying. "After all, we've spent thousands of dollars for Jim's flight training. [As if the Lord didn't already know this!] God, there must be some mistake."

Then in the midst of turmoil, through prayer and reading His Word, God gave me a wonderful peace. He was in control. He had everything—Jim's health, our future—in His hands. Somehow I knew that God would take care of everything. And He did, in a most amazing way.

First He gave me the gift of two Scriptures that are a great comfort in the time of crisis. (You may want to memorize them.) One is Romans 6:13: ". . . give yourselves completely to God—every part of you—to be used for his good purposes." Isn't that exciting? There is nothing to fear. God wants to use us for His *good* purposes, as He is a wonderful and loving God.

The other verse is Romans 12:12: "Be glad for all God is planning for you . . . ." He doesn't make accidents at all. He allows them, yes, but everything that happens to you is for a purpose. He has a plan for *your* life. God does not allow anything in our lives except what has been previewed first by Him. Then He allows it. No matter how circumstances appear to you in the present, you are to be glad, for God is planning good things for you.

The language of trust is "Thank you." The language of believing is "Thank you." And soon I was learning to express my gratitude for the wonderful life He had in store for us after the accident. As a result of Jim's surgeries, I went to work as the director of a new modeling school in Eugene, Oregon.

While living in Eugene, I became Mrs. Oregon—which led me into a lot of hard work and some truly thrilling experiences. The Mrs. America pageant helped open my eyes further to the real needs of women. I realized more than ever before how essential it was to share the way to become inwardly beautiful. "Many women are spending hours of their time and countless dollars without achieving the loveliness they want so deeply," I thought. "How can they become beautiful by applying makeup and hair conditioners, when their souls are in despair?" I knew that homes were breaking up and lives were lived in frustration because women lacked Christ.

Soon I submitted my resignation to the modeling school and devised a course that put God first. And The Image of Loveliness was born. We now live in Salem, Oregon, and my husband is the executive director in charge of our franchise program—both in the United States and abroad. We teach eight three-hour weekly classes, instructing on not only skin care; hair care; diet and nutrition; exercise; etiquette; conversation; posture, wardrobe selection and coordination; but we also spend time on personality improvement by exposing our students to the freedom of loving themselves and others as a result of knowing Jesus Christ personally and following His teachings.

How to Say Yes!

If there were only one thing that I could share with you, it would be to encourage you to get involved in a personal relationship with God. *He loves you unconditionally!*

It may be that you have not yet asked God to come into your life. Perhaps you memorized John 3:16 as a child: "For God so loved the world that he gave his only Son, that whoever believes in him should not perish but have eternal life'' (RSV). And you know about John 10:10, in which Jesus tells us that He came in order that we might have life and have it abundantly. But perhaps you don't really understand what abundant life means, nor do you realize that if you invite Him in, you will become beautiful from the inside out and experience a fullness to your life.

Christ is waiting patiently and lovingly outside your heart's door, "Look! I have been standing at the door and I am constantly knocking. If anyone hears me calling him and opens the door, I will come in and fellowship with him and he with me" (Revelation 3:20).

Ask in faith, believing that He will come in! That's all you have to do, and He will do the rest. "For by grace you have been saved through faith; and this is not your own doing, it is the gift of God—not because of your works, lest any man should boast" (Ephesians 2:8, 9 RSV).

This asking in faith and receiving God's free gift is what is known as "salvation," and whether or not it sounds fashionable, every living person needs it. You may want to close your eyes right at this moment and pray this prayer:

"Lord Jesus, I believe You are God's Son, who died on the cross in my place for my sins. Thank You for forgiving me of my sins. I open the door of my heart and my life, and receive You as my Lord and Saviour. I know that I need You; I've tried so many other things. Take control of this life and heart of mine, and make me the kind of person You want me to be. Show me what true beauty really is all about. Thank You for coming into my heart and life, just as You promised you would."

Do stop reading. Let God speak to you, right now.

Changing

How thankful I will be to know that you have given your life to Jesus Christ. How you will change as the years go by and God works His wonders in you.

The changes in my life were not instantaneous. My problems were years in developing. It took God a while to undo the mess I had made. And God is not through with me yet, as there are still many good lessons to learn.

The Christian life is not an escape or an easy way out. Many new

Christians have been misled to believe that Chrsitianity is "no pain, no strain." Soon they are disillusioned. But God is the overseer. He loves us so much and desires for us to be conformed to His own glorious image! So through laughter and tears, pleasant times and pain, exhilaration and fatigue, we will grow into God's beautiful women.

God is interested in every detail of our lives! How lovingly He watches over us and cares for us. The Psalmist wrote:

"You saw me before I was born and scheduled each day of my life before I began to breathe. Every day was recorded in your Book! How precious it is, Lord, to realize that you are thinking about me constantly! I can't even count how many times a day your thoughts turn towards me. And when I waken in the morning, you are still thinking of me!" (Psalms 139:16–18).

After Thorealdsen had completed his very famous statue of Christ, he brought a friend of his to see it. In the statue, Christ's arms are extended, with His head hanging between His arms.

"But I cannot see Christ's face," said Thorealdsen's friend.

The great sculptor smiled gently. "If you would see the face of Christ, you must get on your knees," he replied.

If you would be beautiful, find a quiet time every day when you can read God's word and pray to Him. *He is interested in you.*

"But they that wait upon the Lord shall renew their strength. They shall mount up with wings like eagles; they shall run and not be weary; they shall walk and not faint" (Isaiah 40:31).

One way in which I am learning to stay close to God throughout the day is to pray, as my friend Bob Hobson has shared: "Lord, I give You my total consent to live in me today. And thank You, Lord."

How I pray that you, too, will make this daily decision. With God's presence you can become the image of loveliness. Yes, that is what God wants you to be: you—a woman—a handmade original—created in the image of God to fulfill a wonderful plan. You—a woman—God's idea!

May he be pleased by all these thoughts about him, for he is the source of all my joy.
                                                    Psalms 104:34

If you are interested in taking the Image of Loveliness course, or becoming a franchised teacher, write to Joanne Wallace for information. The author is also available to speak at seminars, retreats and other gatherings. The address is:

Joanne Wallace
The Image of Loveliness, Inc.
P.O. Box 5162
Salem, Oregon 97304